Who defines THE PUBLIC INTEREST?

edited by TOM FRAME

Copyright Notice

All rights reserved. Apart from any fair dealing for the purposes of private study, research, brief quotations embodied in critical articles or reviews as permitted under the Australian Copyright Act (1968), no part of this work may be reproduced by electronic or other means without the written permission of the publisher. The copyright in individual chapters remains with the respective authors.

Published in 2018 by Connor Court Publishing

Connor Court Publishing Pty Ltd
PO Box 7257
Redland Bay QLD 4165
sales@connorcourt.com

www.connorcourtpublishing.com.au

Phone 0497 900 685

ISBN: 9781925826234

Cover and layout by Graham Lindsay

Printed in Australia

Who defines THE PUBLIC INTEREST?

edited by TOM FRAME

Contents

Preface			vii
Contributors			xii
Introduction		Tom Frame	1
Part 1			
	1	Setting the scene	John McMillan	20
	2	The public interest and the common good: synonymous or a subset	Andrew Cameron	35
Part 2			
	3	Public interest as an accountability test	Chris Wheeler	52
	4	The public interest: the essence of public leadership	Tom Frame	71
Part 3			
	5	The public interest: the exclusive preserve of government?	David Kemp	87
	6	Public interest and political parties	Rodney Cavalier	102
Part 4			
	7	The public interest and public sector priorities	John Uhr	115
	8	Balancing competing: public interests within the public sector	Geoff Gallop	130
Part 5			
	9	The public interest and media reporting	Shaun Carney	144
	10	Public interest and disciplinary communities	Jane Johnston	156
		Postscript	Tom Frame	173

Disclaimer

The views expressed by contributors are their own opinions and do not necessarily represent the position of the Commonwealth of Australia, the New South Wales Government, the University of New South Wales, the University of Queensland, the Australian National University, Charles Sturt University or any organisations with which the contributors were or are now associated. The publication of their chapter in this book does not imply any official agreement or formal concurrence with any opinion, criticism, conclusion or recommendation attributed to them.

Preface

This collection of essays resulted from a conversation with Chris Wheeler, one of the New South Wales Deputy Ombudsman. I had read his work on the challenges he and his colleagues were facing in applying a public interest test to the policies and decisions of parliamentarians and public servants. He identified both the semantic difficulties and the practical problems associated with a term that was readily used but poorly understood. As the new research group I was heading at UNSW Canberra was concerned with public leadership and I believed that the public interest was its focus, we quickly recognised converging interests. The university could gain from his practical experience and the Ombudsman's office would benefit from our scholarly research. Some form of collaboration seemed timely because the term public interest was being increasingly cited by policy makers and administrators to justify and explain their thoughts and actions. There were naturally sceptics including commentators who thought the public interest was being used to mask special pleading. Indeed, just before we talked about a jointly hosted symposium, the whole notion of the public interest being used as a test of individual integrity and personal probity for those holding public office was disparaged in a high-profile court case.

In appealing his conviction for misconduct in public office, lawyers for the gaoled former New South Wales Labor minister Eddie Obeid told the court that the trial judge had erred in telling the jury that as a parliamentarian Obeid was required to act solely in the public interest and not in pursuit of his own financial gain. Guy Reynolds SC argued that the judge could only give that direction to the jury if acting in the public interest was a matter of law. Reynolds insisted that it was 'a mere matter of conscience' and 'a duty of imperfect obligation'. Voters, rather than the courts, should decide whether Obeid had acted in their interests. Obeid's legal counsel went further in contending that acting in the public interest was 'like a duty to be nice to your mum'. The public interest was a political matter of interest to the parliament and not something for the courts to determine. Reynolds contended: 'You breach a duty or an obligation of this kind at your peril if you're an MP because you run the risk that you will or your party will lose at the ballot box'.

Five judges of the New South Wales Court of Criminal Appeal, including Chief Justice Tom Bathurst, were unanimous in rejecting Obeid's claim that the sentence was unjust. The judges noted that when Obeid committed the offence in 2007 he had been in parliament for 16 years and had been a minister for four years. The Chief Justice remarked: 'it is inconceivable that a politician of that standing and experience did not know that his duty was to serve the public interest and that he was not elected to use his position to advance his own or his family's pecuniary interests'. Obeid's subsequent appeal to the High Court in relation to his legal expenses was also rejected. If it were possible for Senior Counsel to refer to the public interest in this dismissive way, there was a need to demonstrate that the term had cogency and coherence. But more than that, it was actually an indispensable concept when it came to defining the purposes of public administration and describing the essence of public service.

The symposium was held over two days in May 2018. The presentations promoted vigorous discussion and very productive debate. They have been enlarged and edited for this collection. I am grateful to my UNSW colleagues Andrew Blyth, Annette Carter and Trish Burgess for organising the symposium, the UNSW Canberra Creative Media Unit for producing the symposium booklets and recording the proceedings, the New South Wales Ombudsman Michael Barnes and his staff, especially Chris Wheeler, for their support and goodwill, and Graham Lindsay and Anthony Capello for their experience and expertise in typesetting the text and designing the book. The overall quality of this publication will be judged by the weakest chapter. I don't believe there are any weak chapters. In fact, I am grateful to all the contributors for their diligence and dedication in submitting work that was a delight to read and a pleasure to edit. Although my name appears on the front cover I hope they all feel a sense of ownership of the whole volume. I am personally grateful to them all.

Tom Frame
Public Leadership Research Group
UNSW Canberra
October 2018

Contributors

Associate Professor Andrew Cameron

Andrew has been a priest in the Anglican Church of Australia since 1993 and has had pastoral experience in a variety of Anglican and other denominational settings. He has also taught in ethics, social ethics, political and public theology, theological anthropology, theology and philosophy at a range of levels and institutions. His doctoral research was a theological account of the relationship of ethics to emotion. Since then he has researched several other topics at the intersection of theology, ethics and public life. He became the Director of St Mark's National Theological Centre and Associate Professor in the School of Theology at Charles Sturt University in 2014.

Adjunct Associate Professor Shaun Carney

Shaun Carney is a columnist with the Herald Sun and has covered Australian governments from Malcolm Fraser to Scott Morrison. He began his career as a journalist in 1978 with *The Herald* in Melbourne where he was a Canberra correspondent and chief industrial relations reporter. He was associate editor and national political columnist with The Age from 1996–2012. In 2003 he received a commendation from the Walkley Award judges for his columns in *The Age*. On leaving *The Age* in 2012, he was appointed an Adjunct Associate Professor in the School of Social Sciences at Monash University and later in the School of Humanities and Social Sciences at UNSW Canberra. His work has appeared in many publications including The Guardian, the Sydney Morning Herald and Rolling Stone. He is the author of *Australia in Accord – Politics and Industrial Relations under the Hawke Government* (1988), *Peter Costello – the New Liberal* (2001) and a memoir, *Press Escape* (2016).

Rodney Cavalier AO

Rodney Cavalier was elected as a Labor member of the New South Wales Parliament in 1978 and served later as a minister in the portfolios of Energy, Finance and Education. Prior to his election to Parliament, Rodney was employed as a trade union official with the Federated Miscellaneous Workers' Union (1972–1973) and was an adviser to the Federal Minister for Labour (1973). Following 10 years in parliament he worked in a number of government-appointed positions including Trustee of the Sydney Cricket Ground Trust. In 2010 he wrote *Power Crisis: the Self Destruction of a State Labor Party*. A further book, *Bronzed: the Basil Sellers SCG Sports Sculptures Project*, was published in 2013. He was chairman of The Sydney Cricket and Sports Ground Trust from 2001 – 2014 and was appointed an Officer of the Order of Australia (AO) in 2004.

Professor Tom Frame

Tom Frame joined the RAN College in 1979 and served in the Navy for 15 years. He was the Anglican Bishop to the Australian Defence Force from 2001–2007 and then Director of St Mark's National Theological Centre from 2007–2014. He served as the Director of the Australian Centre for the Study of Armed Conflict and Society (ACSACS) at UNSW Canberra from 2014 before being appointed founding Director of the UNSW Canberra Public Leadership Research Group-Howard Library in 2017. He is the author or editor of more 40 books including *Living by the Sword: the Ethics of Armed Intervention*; *Moral Injury: Unseen Wounds in an Age of Barbarism*; and *Widening Minds: UNSW and the Education of Australia's Defence Leaders*.

Emeritus Professor Geoff Gallop AC

Geoff was awarded a doctorate in Political Science from Oxford University in 1983. He subsequently pursued a political career as a Member of the Western Australian Legislative Assembly for twenty years until 2006. During this time he was a Government Minister (1990 to 1993), Leader of the Opposition (1996 to 2001), and State Premier (2001 to 2006), his contribution recognised by being awarded a Companion of the Order of Australia (AC) in 2008.

After retiring from politics Geoff became the Director of Sydney University's Graduate School of Government, a position he held until 2015. He currently chairs the Research Committee of the New Democracy Foundation, and continues to contribute to academia as an Emeritus Professor at Sydney University and Adjunct Professor at The John Curtin Institute of Public Policy.

Associate Professor Jane Johnston

Jane Johnston is an Associate Professor in the School of Communication and Arts at the University of Queensland. Jane's research extends across critical public relations, communication and justice, and media diversity and change. She has published widely about the interface between courts and the media, most recently examining how social media has impacted on communication practice. Her most recent research investigates intersections in the public interest with communication and public relations, with publications including *Public Relations and the Public Interest* (2016) and the *Public Interest Communication: Critical Debates and Global Perspectives* (co-edited with Magda Pieczka, 2018). She is the author or editor of two successful public relations books which have both been published in multiple editions: *Public Relations: Theory and Practice* (co-edited first with Clara Zawawi, then Mark Sheehan); and *Media Relations: Issues and Strategies*. Johnston sits on several journal editorial boards and is a regular contributor to the news media.

The Honourable Dr David Kemp AC

David Kemp was a Cabinet Minister in the Howard Government, holding portfolios in the areas of Education and the Environment. He served as federal member for Goldstein (1990–2004). He was Professor of Politics at Monash University (1979–1990), President of the Victorian Division of the Liberal Party of Australia (2007–2011). He is currently chair of the Museum of Australian Democracy at Old Parliament House, chair of the Australian Heritage Council and a board member of the Grattan Institute for Public Policy. He has a doctorate from Yale University in Political Science and is the author of several works including *Society and Electoral Behaviour in Australia* and *Foundations for Australian Political Analysis*. He edited and introduced T*he Forgotten People and Other Studies in*

Democracy and authored the chapter 'The Political Philosophy of Robert Menzies' in JR Nethercote's edited volume, Menzies and the Shaping of Modern Australia. In 2017 he was appointed a Companion of the Order of Australia (AC).

Emeritus Professor John McMillan AO

John McMillan is an Emeritus Professor at the Australian National University where he taught administrative and constitutional law from 1983–2003. He is a co-author of *Control of Government Action: Text, Cases and Commentary*. John has held the statutory positions of Commonwealth Ombudsman (2003–10), Integrity Commissioner (Acting) for the Australian Commission for Law Enforcement Integrity (2007), Australian Information Commissioner (2010–15), New South Wales Ombudsman (Acting) (2015–17), and member of the Australian Copyright Tribunal (2015–18). John is a National Fellow of the Institute of Public Administration Australia, a Fellow of the Australian Academy of Law, an honorary life member of the Australian Institute of Administrative Law, and recipient of the Lifetime Achievers Award from the Society of Consumer Affairs Professionals. John was made an Officer of the Order of Australia (AO) in 2010.

Professor John Uhr

John Uhr is Professor of Political Science at the Australian National University (ANU). Awarded an international Commonwealth Scholarship, John completed a Masters degree and PhD in political science at the University of Toronto, Canada. He was later awarded a Harkness Fellowship and spent two years in Washington, DC at the Brookings Institution studying policy and public administration. John has worked in the Australian parliament as a Senate committee secretary and has taught political theory and Australian politics at the ANU since 1990. He has directed the ANU Parliamentary Studies Centre and more recently the Centre for the Study of Australian Politics. His publications include the recent book *Performing Political Theory* (2018) and before that *Prudential Public Leadership* (2015). Among his co-authored books are *Leadership Performance and Rhetoric* (2017) and several co-edited books, including *Eureka: Australia's Greatest Story* (2015), *Studies in Australian Political Rhetoric* (2014), *How Power Changes Hands* (2011), *Public Leadership* (2008). Earlier books include

Deliberative Democracy in Australia (1998) and *Terms of Trust: arguments over ethics in Australian government* (2005).

Chris Wheeler

Chris Wheeler has been a New South Wales Deputy Ombudsman since 1994. He has over 30 years' experience in complaint handling and investigations, as well as extensive experience in management and public administration. Chris has responsibility for the public administration area of the Ombudsman's office, including public interest disclosure. He also has responsibility for major research projects (including the management of Unreasonable Complainant Conduct), and the development of guidance materials to assist public sector agencies and officials to achieve and maintain good practice in relation to complaint handling, public administration and conduct generally.

INTRODUCTION

The public interest: problems and possibilities

Tom Frame

When a public figure claims that an action has been taken in the public interest, members of the public are encouraged, if not exhorted, to believe the action reflects a higher motivation and embodies a superior spirit; that it transcends personal aspiration and private gain; and, that it deserves to be recognised as an expression of altruism serving the greater good and deserving of respect. Because the term 'public interest' has a near sacred resonance, it is employed to justify, if not ennoble, a wide range of assertions and affirmations, declarations and decisions.

The first difficulty with assessing assertions of the public interest is the absence of an agreed definition. In some instances, governments have concluded that the public interest cannot be readily defined or that attempted definitions would be counterproductive or antithetical to advancing the public interest. For instance, the Information and Privacy Commission in New South Wales has issued a fact sheet explaining that all government agencies must disclose or release information unless there is an overriding public interest against disclosure, with decisions on whether to disclose or release information guided by the 'Public Interest Test'.[1] The test consists of three steps, each of which involves 'public interest considerations'. These considerations are not explained although five relevant factors are described briefly. These factors include 'promoting open discussion of public affairs' and 'contributing to positive and informed debate on issues of public importance'. These factors purportedly serve the public interest although how and why is left unexplained.

The United Kingdom Ministry of Defence has adopted a similar public interest test for the release of information. Its 'Guidance Note' on the test makes the point that 'public authorities act on behalf of the public as a whole – in the public interest – not in the name of, or on behalf of, individuals or private interests'.[2] There are several subsequent references to the 'public as a whole' as the entity to whom the public interest relates but, the note states, 'there is no definition of public interest (or of 'harm') in the relevant legislation relating to the release of information'. The absence of a definition is to allow officials 'to conduct a specific analysis in the light of the current circumstances, rather than being constrained by set criteria'. Apparently, the public interest in 'a particular piece of information' might change over time requiring the consideration of different factors. Thus, the 'assessment of the public interest is a judgement in which fact, policy and law are all involved to some degree'. There is, however, one clarification: 'Public interest is not the same as what the public is interested in – public curiosity about a subject is not the same as the public interest favouring the release of information'. The note is nonetheless clear that 'the release of information serves the public interest if it will enhance accountability or prevent harm'.

Where there have been attempts at a definition, they are problematic. *Butterworth's Australian Legal Dictionary* defines the term as 'an interest in common to the public at large or a significant portion of the public and which may, or may not, involve the personal or propriety rights of individual people'.[3] This definition is unhelpful. It is vague, imprecise and open to so many interpretations as to render it practically useless.

During the month spent drafting this introduction (April–May 2018), I collected every media report mentioning the public interest. My initial fear was a dearth of reports and I would be left with nothing to compare and contrast. The opposite was true. There were at least a dozen media reports (all from Australian media outlets) on a range of topics that made reference to the public interest in different contexts. I selected the six most detailed stories from those collected although I was looking for a common element. In each instance they featured assertions of the public interest where the authority of an institution or an individual to define the public interest was assumed rather than argued. In their own way, each demonstrated the assumption that an organisation or an official possessed the authority to assert or an entitlement to define the public interest. Further, these individuals presume their judgement is fair-minded, imply their assessments are non-partisan and, in speaking for the majority of citizens, beyond challenge or above contradiction. There was an inference in each instance that the complexities associated with claiming the public interest could be overlooked and that, in some circumstances, the public are not always entitled to know the basis on which their interests are being protected or promoted. Finally, every assertion of the public interest was made in the sure and certain knowledge that it transcended all other interests in both credibility and criticality.

The entitlement to define the public interest is a foundational question in deliberations over public policy. There is, however, scant regard for the importance of cogency in claiming a policy advances or an action embodies the public interest and there is near indifference to consistency in the making of such claims despite the need for them to be persuasive and trustworthy if they are to be taken seriously. Before any public interest claim is subjected to rigorous scrutiny, the standing of the claimant and their entitlement to speak for the public needs to be verified to ensure such claims are not treated with either uncritical acceptance or unjustified contempt. In the following case studies, readers are invited to focus on the identity and affiliation of the individual making a claim for the public interest, the ease with which they claimed much wider support for their claim, the readiness with which the public are recruited to their cause and the conviction accompanying their identification of interests. Each instance relies on rhetorical 'sleight of hand' to avoid accusations that the claims being made are actually self-interested on the part of individuals or a form of special pleading where an institution is involved.

Case study 1

On 26 March 2018, the media reported that the Immigration Minister, Peter Dutton, had granted a foreign *au pair* a visa after the young woman's bid to enter Australia was ruled unlawful. Her E-visitor visa was cancelled at the Brisbane airport on 17 June 2015 rendering her an 'unlawful non-citizen' under migration laws. The minister then intervened although we do not know at whose behest. He later explained: 'Having regard to this person's particular circumstances and personal characteristics, I have decided to exercise my discretionary powers ... as it would be in the public interest to grant this person a visa'. The minister declined to explain why or how the public interest was served by granting a visa to this woman although he denied knowing the *au pair* before confirming she did not work for him or his family. A decision taken in the public interest was not explained to the public in whose interests the minister claimed to be acting. Subsequent media reporting revealed that Dutton had acted contrary to the advice of his department amid allegations that he exercised ministerial discretion at the request of individuals who were known personally to him. In essence, he is alleged to have intervened to help friends and Liberal party donors. The basis of Dutton's claim to have acted in the public interest has still not been disclosed.

Case study 2

On 4 April 2018, the then Federal Minister for Energy, Josh Frydenberg, commenting on the consequences of closing the Liddell coal-fired power station in the Hunter Valley, argued that selling the plant 'would prolong its life and be in the public interest'. In this instance the public interest appeared to take the form of readily available and competitive priced electrical power and the need for Government intervention to prevent the market becoming 'dysfunctional'.[4] The same day, the then Prime Minister Malcolm Turnbull urged the Chairman of AGL to keep the Liddell power station operating until 2027 because 'it's in the public interest, it's in the community's interest'. The prime minister claimed the Government was not 'picking sides in a commercial dispute' because 'our interest and the public interest' happened to coincide in ensuring power availability after Liddell's scheduled closure in 2022. In this instance according to the prime minister, the interests of AGL shareholders should be subordinated to the public interest as a matter of corporate conscience and commercial goodwill. The prime minister implied the Commonwealth Government was custodian of the national interest and that, as the nation's leader, he was in a position to declare where the public interest lay without fear of contradiction. He made no mention of contrary opinions that were arguing for reduced reliance on coal-fired power stations and he presumed that the cost and availability of power were the only factors to be considered.

Case study 3

On 6 April 2018, the former Prime Minister John Howard claimed the proposed amalgamation of the construction and maritime unions failed a 'public interest' test and criticised the Turnbull Government for failing to legislate after promising to do so in 2016. The merger allegedly represented the 'ultra-concentration of union power' creating an organisation that would, according to Mr Howard, be 'cashed up and super militant'. As the merger of BHP and Billiton had been subjected to a public interest test applied by a regulator (in this instance, the Australian Competition and Consumer Commission) to ensure the new entity would not weaken competition in the mining industry, consistency apparently demanded that union mergers face the same kind of scrutiny to ensure a super union did not secure sufficient power to harm the national interest. Howard's assertions of the public interest were taken at face value. No objection was raised to his party political affiliation or ideological convictions, his long-term suspicion of organised labour and his record on workplace relations reform (such as *Workchoices*), or Australia's obligations under International Labour Organisation conventions with respect to worker organisations. His views were given prominence because of his status as a former prime minister and without due regard to the democratic rights of workers to organise or the consequences of prohibiting the amalgamation on more general rights of free association.

Case study 4

On 9 April 2018, Paul Kerin, Adjunct Professor of Economics at Adelaide University, writing in the *Australian* was critical of the Monash Forum's 'Coalist Manifesto'.[5] The Monash Forum is a faction within the parliamentary Liberal party that included former Prime Minister Tony Abbott and backbench energy committee chair Craig Kelly. Kerin alleged the then Prime Minister Malcolm Turnbull was to blame for a document Kerin described as 'nuts'. He then commented: 'Rather than make 'first-best' policy choices that serve the public interest …. once some 'second-best' policy choices – such as the Renewable Energy Target – were made … the end result is a third-rate mess that serves no-one's best interests'. He concluded with a plea for 'the basic principles of evidence-based policymaking'. Kerin claimed the ability and the capacity to define the public interest because he was an academic with sound and relevant credentials, an apolitical policy analyst committed to evidence over assertion, who assumed his contribution would be seen as even-handed and conscientious. In support of his non-partisan credentials, Kerin could have mentioned that he resigned from a government regulatory oversight position in South Australia after the Labor Party was re-elected in 2013, citing its partisan approach to energy policy. His criticisms of the Federal government implied that the public interest would not be served by the operation of market forces but only by direct government intervention.

Case study 5

On 11 April 2018, the *Adelaide Advertiser* reported that whistleblowers would be afforded greater protection when they report corruption and wrongdoing as the incoming South Australian State Government was intending to draft journalist shield laws. [South Australia and Queensland were the only states without shield laws designed to allow journalists to keep their sources confidential.] The draft legislation would apply in instances where refusing to name the source of information was clearly in the public interest. Judges would, however, be able to compel the disclosure where a greater good was served in discovering the informant's identity. The courts could only set aside the protections if the benefits to the community outweighed any negative impact on the informant, the free flow of information and the value of maintaining a free press. The Government said the change was intended to cover South Australia's Independent Commission Against Corruption, despite the agency not being identified in the draft legislation. Under the new law, the judiciary was empowered to determine the public interest in the context of many competing interests – including the authority and the standing of the judiciary in political and social affairs. In this instance, the Government had identified an area of public interest that it wanted to advance but would leave the actual determination of the public interest to the courts and judicial officers.

Case study 6

On 27 April 2018, the Director General of the Australian Secret Intelligence Service (ASIS), former Major General Paul Symon, appeared at the Administrative Appeals Tribunal (AAT) to argue the agency should not be required to release documents relating to covert Australia intelligence gathering in East Timor after the Indonesian invasion in 1975 including information held about the murder of five Australian journalists at Balibo in October of that year. The Acting Attorney General, Greg Hunt, had previously been persuaded to allow ASIS to present its evidence and arguments 'in camera'. Hunt stated: 'disclosure of this information would be contrary to the public interest by reason that it would prejudice the security, defence or international relations of Australia'. Consequently, Hunt issued a 'public interest certificate to protect the information'. The reasons for the material being withheld would not be made public, preventing any counter-argument being made by academics or the families of the dead journalists who were requesting the access. A relative of the 'Balibo Five', Greg Cunningham, commented: 'all we need is the truth. We are not after justice … we just want to be told what happened [at Balibo]'. The public interest was conflated with the national interest and was, according to Symon and Hunt, inconsistent with the professional interest of academics and the personal interest of families. Notably, the public interest being protected was itself withheld from public scrutiny, ironically, in the public interest.

Who defines the public interest?

In the media reporting of these case studies, the first issue canvassed is not the authority of those making claims about the public interest but the essence of the claims. There was no discussion of the standing or status of the claimants in relation to the matters at hand. The presenting issue seemed to be the refusal of an individual or organisation to acknowledge and accept a public interest claim when, in each instance, legitimate questions could be asked about whether the claimant is acting from self or sectional-interest, whether the claimant is technically competent to pronounce on an issue, and whether they have the perspective necessary to speak confidently on behalf of the public.

In each of these case studies, the government and its representatives asserted a unilateral entitlement to determine the public interest without needing to identify the distinct publics or the interests it was presuming to protect or promote. In two instances, claims by government officials to be acting in the public interest were neither explained nor justified. In one instance, the argument was circular and self-serving: the government did not believe it was in the public interest to explain the public interest being served. When the reasons for a public interest decision are not disclosed, the public are naturally entitled to be suspicious and sceptical. The consequences of repeatedly refusing to explain decisions are profound. Not only is trust in government reduced, the value of the public interest as a test of good policy and sound decision-making is diminished.

The case studies also revealed the curious presumption that the absence of a direct personal interest allowed an individual to pronounce on the public interest while the possibility of such an individual being influenced by a vested interest remained was overlooked. In all of the case studies, the public being served is never described and the interests being served are never disclosed other than the inference that they are individual interests or collective interests in which individuals have a stake. Most surprising is the ease and rapidity with which the public interest is identified and determined, implying the claimant either speaks confidently on behalf of the public or knows with assurance what the public needs. One thing is, however, very clear. There is little consensus on who defines the public interest and the basis of their authority to do so.

The question 'who defines the public interest?' reveals a substantial challenge for those who believe the public interest is the cornerstone of good public policy and the wellspring of effective public leadership. Put simply: other than thinking that parliamentarians define the public interest because they are elected by the public to serve their interests, there is considerable discussion about the role of ministerial advisers, political parties, public servants, lobby groups, media presenters and university academics in discerning the community's mood and defining the public interest. There has been very little attention to the role of not-for-profit organisations and businesses in defining the public interest although both provide products and services that are consumed by the public in pursuit of their interests.

If the government declines for whatever reason to provide a service, a private organisation might decide to offer such a service in the public interest. The government might decide that it doesn't need to provide a service because the private sector is able to meet the needs of the community effectively and efficiently through the operation of the market. Animal welfare is in the public interest but serving this interest is delegated to a not-for-profit organisation – the RSPCA. The provision of experienced and expert medical care is in the public interest but the certification of suitable practitioners is the responsibility of an industry group – the AMA. In addition to parliamentarians, thousands of people are making millions of decisions everyday that are intended to serve the public interest. The authority of these people to make such decisions is rarely questioned because they cannot do their jobs without deciding that something advances or retards the interests of the public. They make decisions conscious of the public interest because their duty statement requires them to do so or they protect or promote the public interest because they discern it is the right thing to do and should be done.

An individual commitment to act always and everywhere in the public interest is widely considered a noble sentiment worthy of praise. But a desire to act in the public interest must confront a number of challenges. What happens when the public's interests are unclear? Who will adjudicate on rival claims about where the public's first or best interests might lie? These are not new questions. They are foundational to all political discourse if we see politics as a contest of ideas or a competition of interests. Curiously, these matters have not attracted as much attention as their importance would suggest they deserve. In fact, very few discussions of the public interest begin with what ought to be the first question: who has the authority to make claims with respect to the public interest.

A notable exception is a report entitled *Acting in the Public Interest: A Framework for Analysis* produced by the Institute of Chartered Accountants in England and Wales (ICAEW) in 2012. The seven-stage framework for acting in the public interest, starts with 'credentials for the invoking of the public interest'.

> Asserting that an action is in the public interest involves setting oneself up in judgment as to whether the action or requirement to change behaviour will benefit the public overall – a far greater set of people than can be interacted with directly. It involves interference in people's ability to go about their business or sometimes, as a positive policy decision, non-interference in the face of alternative actions.[6]

Although concerns about the public interest usually involved 'organisations seeking to change people's actions through laws, regulations or other methods of persuasion' it helpfully noted that' 'individuals can intervene by taking public interest actions themselves, for example by overriding confidentiality requirements to disclose bad behaviour by others'. The report recognised that 'invoking the public interest requires justification of an ability and right to decide what is for the greater good, in the face of a natural suspicion that those proposing an action in the public interest are actually acting in their own interests'.

The foremost credential for invoking the public interest is trust because 'the rationale for invoking the public interest generally involves persuasion and justification, and that justification influences the amount of trust engendered in the relevant public. This in turn affects the effectiveness of the persuasion'. After noting increasing levels of distrust in those holding positions of authority, the report pointed to evidence suggesting a growing presumption

> that invoking the public interest is a smokescreen to disguise self-interested action, whether deliberately or subconsciously. It is helpful, therefore, for proponents of public interest actions to consider what the key threats to trust by the relevant public might be (for example, conflicts of interest) as well as threats to making the right decision (for example, past mistakes).

For the validity of an assertion of the public interest to be generally accepted, the public must trust in the integrity and judgment of its leaders. Building the requisite trust may need to overcome past instances of professional incompetence, poor judgment and technical mistakes; corruption, bribery or failure to recognise conflicts of interest.

The ICAEW was especially concerned with devolving the setting and monitoring of public standards to professional organisations and industry regulators when such bodies may not be fully representative and could be captured by sectional interests. It noted that public choice theory contends that general self-interest incentives from the market place continue to apply to people in the public and regulatory sectors. George Stigler's 'economic theory of regulation', first enunciated in 1971, argues that demand for legislation usually originates with interest groups who would expect to benefit from its provisions.[7] Popularly elected governments, which seek to maximise their electoral support in the hope of perpetuating their political power, have authority to initiate and enact legislation that allow them to apply coercive force and assert regulatory power. It follows, according to Stigler, that state control arises not so much in the presence of market imperfections but where an interest group is able to offer the decision-makers something worthwhile – the ability to increase their appeal to sections of the electorate whose support they do presently enjoy or cannot afford to alienate.

Given the propensity of public interest claims to be specious and self-serving, why does the public interest need to be invoked at all? Is it invoked too often or too readily? The ICAEW proposes a number of safeguards, including a checklist or aide memoire, which can be used by individuals and organisations for the identification of possible self-interest. As might be expected of an accounting organisation, the ICAEW offers an approach to cost-benefit analysis that would assist in testing public interest claims with respect to competing policy options that involve investment of money or labour. The report concludes that transparency and accountability are central to the integrity and effectiveness of processes designed to identify, defend or advance the public interest.

Validating public interest claims

While political leaders or government officials might define the public interest, Lok Sang Ho, Professor of Economics at Lingnan University in Hong Kong, argues for another approach in his insightful book *Public Policy and the Public Interest*.[8] He begins by suggesting the 'proper role of government is to serve the people and that public policy should be designed to serve the public interest'. He further suggests that 'governments should be a friend of each person, so that he or she feels protected and able to pursue happiness' although he agrees that governments have an overarching duty to promote the common good which happens by balancing the interests of the diverse groups within a society. This balancing, he cautions, must be minor and 'should not have a material effect on economic and social development as long as the common good is put on the top of the agenda ahead of the minor balancing'.

Professor Ho defines the public interest as the 'interest of the representative individual – an imaginary person who forgot his identity and who imagined that he has an equal chance of being anyone in society'. He continues:

> By pondering policy options using this *ex ante* [translated: literally 'before the event' and paraphrased as 'based on forecasts rather than results'] perspective impartially, the most preferred option is the one that is deemed to maximise the public interest. With the public interest defined this way policy decisions should be made on the basis of comparing benefits in terms of enhancement of the public interest one the one hand, and costs on the other hand.

Ho draws on the work of the British political philosopher John Stuart Mill (1806–1873), the Hungarian-American economist John Harsanyi (1920–2000) and the American moral philosopher John Rawls (1921–2002) who based their methodologies on the judgement of the impartial observer located behind a veil of ignorance, having no sense of their material wealth, their scholastic or practical talents, their preferences or their prejudices, their gender or age, race or religion. Without any form of self-interest being allowed to intrude, the representative individual will *not* know whether they personally stand to gain or lose from public policies and will, therefore, be more likely to decide fairly whether a decision is in the public interest. Notably, Harsanyi's approach was to maximise the equally weighted sum of individual welfares whereas Rawls is concerned to maximise the welfare of the worst off person. The difference in outlook apparent in the work of Harsanyi and Rawls draws attention to the crucial importance of an interpretative framework during both the design and the delivery – the principles and pragmatics – of public policy.

Discussion of the public interest rightly concentrates on the distorting intrusion of self or sectional interest. There is much less attention to the general values that ought to shape public policy or the common virtues that are critical to its effective and efficient implementation. An individual who has forsaken self-interest or an organisation that has embraced altruism are nonetheless animated by a vision of the things that make for personal happiness and collective prosperity. Professor Ho looks to a self-forgetful person with no past, a symbolic individual without a sense of their own identity and, presumably, without any ideological orientation, to deliberate on the public interest. I readily see the appeal of Ho's approach. It is an attempt to determine the impact of a policy on the total well-being (or happiness) of an ordinary-average-regular member of society. The main factors influencing total well-being are physical, mental, emotional and spiritual, echoing Abraham Maslow's well-known hierarchy of needs. For Ho, the ultimate point of public policy is enhancing individual happiness which he distinguishes from Benthamite utility and its desire to achieve a positive balance of pleasure over pain.

While there is much merit in Ho's approach, I am not completely persuaded by Ho's arguments partly because of the difficulty of reconciling what a representative (or hypothetical) person might believe about the moral structure of human society and the point and purpose of human living, and what someone who has actually wrestled with their own prejudices and preferences really believes. In considering the public interest, we need to deal not with possible beliefs drawn from depersonalised analysis but real convictions built on hard-earned wisdom and insight. We must also be mindful of the very real possibility that a selfless individual, even Professor Ho's self-forgetful person, could be mistaken, deluded or unable to decide about the efficacy of competing claims about where the public interest might reside in relation to any aspect of human living. Personal identity shapes individual destiny and, therefore, guides the decisions that people might make about furthering their self-interest and the interests of the society in which they have a stake.

We also need to be mindful of the dynamic nature of political life and the, at times, rapidly changing aspirations of those who constitute the body politic. No public leader and no private voter are ever convinced that every aspect of the common life of a society exists in a state of harmony, equilibrium or balance. Depending upon their political credo, elected leaders and public officials (who often have considerable discretion to interpret policy and legislation) will look for ways consistent with their ideological beliefs that deal with imbalances that can be addressed and inequities which ought to be removed. In an attempt to tip the balance in favour of one overburdened group or to compensate another group for injustice, policies that 'push the pendulum' too far might be proposed in the knowledge that things will eventually return to a stable mid-point in the future. The redistribution of common wealth often relies on state-sponsored paternalism that would fail a public interest test if the past and the future were to be excluded from consideration.

Conversely as Professor Ross Garnaut observes, there are also 'deceitful versions of the common good' arising from the structural features of Australian democracy:

> The political balance in contests between the public and private interest is never determined simply by the democratic adding machine. Wealth has influence in the political process, whether exercised through donations to political parties, or spending to shape public opinion, or in other ways. The big question ... is whether changes in the way private forces seek to influence policy has removed the possibility of governing in the public interest in the twenty-first century.[9]

He was concerned that the conduct of contemporary politics 'has created an environment in which governments can lose their nerve and do the bidding of private interests' but felt that 'private interests are still not able to block a government with a clear idea of its objectives and which seeks to appeal to the electorate in the name of the public interest'.

Ho's approach might also produce a form of hidden bias. His reliance on the representative individual to deliberate on public interest claims is a variation of the deliberative applied in defamation cases: material is considered libellous if deemed to be so by hypothetical referees variously described as 'the reasonable man' in 1882 by Lord Selbourne, 'right thinking members of society generally' in 1936 by Lord Atkin and 'ordinary men not avid for scandal' in 1964 by Lord Reith. In such cases, the courts decide what meaning the words would have conveyed to an ordinary and reasonable person – an unremarkable representative of the citizenry, applying general knowledge and common sense. The difficulties with this approach are dealt with in Roy Baker's *Defamation Law and Social Attitudes: Ordinary Unreasonable People*. Baker, Lecturer in Law at Macquarie University, examines

> the way in which the law decides whether a publication is defamatory, and the consequences for that process of a phenomenon known as the third-person effect: the tendency for individuals to perceive the adverse impact of a communication as greater on others than on themselves ... [A]s a result of this tendency,

defamation law unnecessarily and unfairly silences speech on the basis of protection to reputation, even though little or no reputational harm would actually occur. What is more, defamation law perpetuates regressive attitudes and could do more to promote a just and inclusive society.[10]

Similarly, there is a substantial likelihood of the 'third-person effect' distorting the assessment of a policy's actual outcome. The issue is not whether an assertion of the public interest is free from self-interest but whether it can be equally distorted by the intrusion of sympathy and charity. While these qualities might be laudable in the conduct of inter-personal relationships, they can harm the development and delivery of effective and sustainable public policy.

✽ ✽ ✽ ✽ ✽ ✽

In addition to canvassing possible visions and practical expressions of the public interest, this volume focuses on the important question: who has authority to assert, and then to act, in the public interest? As the following chapters will show, it is not simply elected leaders or government officials although they have a prominent role. In some instances, private citizens have seized the initiative and asserted their entitlement as members of the public to assert an interest on behalf of others principally through advocacy such as whistleblowing. In addition to discussing who might claim legitimately to define the public interest, this volume examines the limits of public interest claims and how they are expressed in a range of settings.

The contributors represent a range of perspectives that draw on diverse experiences and expertise. Professor John McMillan comes from a legal background and writes with long experience as a senior public servant with responsibility for the oversight of public administration at the state and federal levels. Associate Professor Andrew Cameron is a theologian and ethicist concerned with both the classical and contemporary expression of moral claims and ethical statements. Chris Wheeler draws on his long experience of town planning and regulatory oversight at the state level with first-hand experience of conflicts between governments and private citizens over competing aspirations and debates among government agencies over due process. My contribution draws on previous academic work in sociology and politics, and interactions with government agencies committed to ethical leadership. Dr David Kemp has been writing about political philosophy, especially the origins and objectives of liberalism, for more than forty years as an academic, ministerial adviser and parliamentarian. Similarly, Rodney Cavalier draws on his deep knowledge of party politics in New South Wales and on his own experience as a minister in the Wran and Unsworth Governments. Professor John Uhr is one of Australia's foremost thinkers on the relationship between politics and public administration, and has produced many books and articles considering the dynamics of public leadership and policy. Emeritus Professor Geoff Gallop combines a distinguished career in state politics drawing on his experience as a minister and later premier with insights drawn from the academic study of democratic structures and their influence on public administration. Associate Professor Shaun Carney is a highly respected journalist who has been faced with the need to make decisions everyday about the stories he will publish and their possible impact on private lives and professional careers. Associate Professor Jane Johnston makes use of her considerable experience in public relations and strategic communications to explore the ways a number of professions and disciplinary communities have understood the broader contribution they can make to human flourishing by focussing on the public interest.

This book is intended to be a resource for students and practitioners of public administration where the concept of the public interest has a central place in guiding decision-making and reconciling rival political claims or competing policy prescriptions. The contributors were chosen because of their experiences, affiliations and disciplines. They have expertise in the federal and state arenas, come from both sides of the political divide and are drawn from a range of intellectual pursuits. As the public interest has not been considered in this way before, the contributors were also conscious of the need to survey the terrain and identify the key questions that still needing addressing. Surprisingly, the public interest as a concept resists quick and easy definitions. Plainly, what could be said about the public interest in one context could not be said in another. This book will not be the last word on the complex and sometimes controversial concept of the public interest. There is much more work to be done. But every journey has to start somewhere. The contributors to this volume have performed an important service. We can now place a pin on a map with the accompanying words: 'You are here'.

Endnotes

1. New South Wales Information and Privacy Commission, 'What is the public interest test?', Fact Sheet, January 2016.
2. Ministry of Defence, Access to Information, Guidance Note E4: the Public Interest Test, version 6, June 2009.
3. See https://austlii.edu.au/austlii/guide/current/20030315--7.html
4. Paul Garvey and Matt Chambers, 'Liddell closure 'risks power market'', *Australian*, 4 April 2018.
5. Paul Kerin, 'Turnbull snow job opens door to coal confusion', *Australian*, 9 April 2018.
6. ICAEW, 'Acting in the Public Interest: a Framework for Analysis', *www.icaew.com/marketfoundations*, first published 2012.
7. George Stigler, 'The Theory of Economic Regulation', *The Bell Journal of Economics and Management Science*, vol. 2, no. 1, Spring 1971, pp. 3–21.
8. Lok Sang Ho, *Public Policy and the Public Interest*, Routledge, Oxford, 2012.
9. Ross Garnaut, *Dog Days: Australia After the Boom*, Redback, Melbourne, 2013, p. 234.
10. A summary of the author's main arguments and principal conclusions can be found in Roy Baker, 'Defamation and the Moral Community', www.austlii.edu.au/au/journals/DeakinLRev/2008/1.pdf.

CHAPTER 1

The public interest – setting the scene

John McMillan

This chapter deals with three broad issues arising from using the term 'public interest'. First, is it a useful concept? What does it mean, and is that meaning contextual and variable? Who defines the public interest in particular settings, and how do they do so?

The widespread common usage of the term 'public interest' points to its popularity and acceptance. What follows are examples of the wide-ranging use of the term in legislation, as a legal concept, in government reports, by public figures, in the media and elsewhere.

Legislation

Public interest is used as an adjectival or qualifying phrase in a large number of statutes. Commonwealth legislation provides a range of examples.

The *Public Interest Disclosure Act 2013* protects public officials who make public interest disclosures (PID) in accordance with the procedures in the Act. A PID is a disclosure of information which the discloser reasonably believes shows that another official engaged in corruption, an abuse of public trust, a perversion of justice, maladministration, or a waste of public assets (section 29).

The *Privacy Act 1988* authorises the Information Commissioner to make a Public Interest Determination that exempts a program (such as medical research) from the operation of privacy regulation (section 72).

The *Social Security (Administration) Act 1999* authorises the Minister to issue a Public Interest Certificate that permits disclosure of personal information that is otherwise confidential (section 208).

The *Freedom of Information Act 1982* uses a public interest balancing test to determine if government policy documents are exempt from disclosure or should be released upon request (section 11B).

Under the *Migration Regulations* an applicant for a migration visa must satisfy Public Interest Criteria to be granted a visa.

The *Telecommunications (Interception and Access) Act 1979* empowers the Prime Minister to appoint a Public Interest Advocate to make submissions on whether a warrant should be issued to allow law enforcement access to a journalist's telecommunications data (section 180X).

Legal concepts

Many of the legal doctrines and principles developed by the courts frequently incorporate a public interest element. Again, there is no shortage of examples. The doctrine of public interest immunity (discussed below) spells out competing public interest considerations that a court will balance in deciding whether government documents are privileged from production in legal proceedings, or must be released to the parties and the court. Unless there is a positive indication in a statute to the contrary, an official who is exercising a broad (or unconfined) statutory discretion can take an undefined range of public interest considerations into account. Public interest considerations are relevant to whether a defamatory statement is justified as a fair comment based on facts relating to a matter of public interest. Public interest considerations are relevant in considering if an adverse costs order should be made against an unsuccessful plaintiff, such as a community organisation. Public interest considerations are relevant to whether a suppression order will be issued to prohibit publication of evidence given in a court proceeding.

Government codes and reports

Government guidance documents frequently refer to the public interest in defining the responsibilities of government and officials. The Australian Public Service Commission publication, *Values and Code of Conduct in Practice*, advises that 'it is ministers who decide what is in the public interest and how it should be brought about' (paragraph 1.3.5), that public servants should 'not pursue a personal view about the public interest' (paragraph 1.9.3), and that 'inappropriate disclosure of information is against the public interest' (paragraph 4.2.1). The Australian Government *Statement of Ministerial Standards* declares that 'Ministers are expected to conduct all official business on the basis that they may be expected to demonstrate publicly that their actions and decisions in conducting public business were taken with the sole objective of advancing the public interest' (section 6.1). The Australian Government *Guidelines for Official Witnesses before Parliamentary Committees* advises officials giving evidence that 'it has been acknowledged by the parliament that the government holds information which, in the public interest, should not be disclosed' (para 4.4.1). The WA Inc. Royal Commission held in 1992 noted that 'government is constitutionally bound to act in the public interest'.[1] The Australian Law Reform Commission report in 2009 on *Secrecy Law and Open Government in Australia* proposed that the criminal law should only penalise unauthorised disclosure of information if it harmed 'essential public interests', such as security, defence, international relations and the protection of public safety (Rec 8–1).

Media reporting

A web search of *The Canberra Times* made in May 2018 identified 6,883 articles in which the term public interest was used. In the preceding week the term was used in articles commenting on business disdain for the public interest, defamation laws blocking public interest stories, the decline of public interest journalism, land valuation for redevelopment being contrary to the public interest, local council public interest development variations, the public interest case for the banking royal commission, and speculative public interest litigation by Eddie McGuire against Facebook for publishing fake advertisements suggesting he used treatments to increase his sexual potency.

Political leaders and public bodies

There are other assorted uses of the public interest. Tom Frame's chapter in this collection gives six case studies of ministers and other public figures relying on the public interest to justify decisions or proposals as diverse as granting a visa, electricity generation arrangements, opposition to union mergers, energy management, media shield laws and intelligence gathering. In New South Wales there is a Public Interest Advocacy Centre. A large number of law schools in the United States now offer postgraduate courses in public interest law, just as many other disciplines offer courses such as public interest health, public interest regulation and public interest accounting.

Defining the concept of public interest

This widespread use of the term public interest underscores the difficulty of adopting any simple or accepted definition. I will expand on that observation in four stages. *First*, use of the phrase is common in all quarters of public life – in law, politics, public administration, the media, in setting public sector priorities, as a facet of leadership expectations, to guide regulatory and disciplinary processes, and in theories of governance and accountability. Use of the term is both infinite and unregulated. Clearly this usage will continue. As one author comments, the concept has become 'an integral part of the discourse, law, regulation and governance of modern democracies'.[2]

Second, if there is a unifying theme it is probably that authors choose the term for effect. They generally use it to pronounce or strengthen some underlying purpose that is thought to be progressive, altruistic or aspirational. Thus, a particular outcome is described as being 'in the public interest'. An activity that is to be suppressed may be characterised as being 'against the public interest'. And it requires special insight or authority, such as that of an elected politician or judge, to decide what the public interest requires in a particular situation.

It is a familiar feature of public discourse that we select phrases or tags to depict a two-dimensional view of public policy outcomes: something is said to be for or against the public interest, when in truth the choice is more complex or multi-faceted. Other phrases that imply a similar dichotomy between acceptable and unacceptable outcomes include 'human rights', 'national interest', 'personal privacy' and 'national security'. An up-and-coming contender to join this list is the political promise that the future response to civil disturbances or law enforcement threats will be 'zero tolerance'!

Another indication that the term public interest is used to elicit support or evoke confidence is that it is not necessarily the most appropriate term for particular usages. The title of the *'Public Interest' Disclosure Act* is misleading to the extent that the scheme of the Act is to encourage internal disclosure: the alternative title for the Act could be the *Whistleblowers Protection Act*. A 'Public Interest' determination or certificate is a statutory instrument that could simply be called a determination or certificate: indeed, the usual purpose of the determination or certificate is to override the operation of legislation that has a public interest objective such as protection of privacy. A 'Public Interest' advocate is a barrister who makes submissions in a closed-door hearing and consults with no-one before advocating a particular viewpoint. 'Public interest' journalism could perhaps describe all journalism rather than a special class of journalism. 'Public interest' litigation is no different to any litigation to the extent that it is initiated by an individual plaintiff against an individual defendant, often with a claim for damages.

Third, the definitional challenge posed by the term public interest is accentuated by the prescription in most usage that there is a shared understanding of what it means or what will be an acceptable outcome. Dictionary definitions go some way in meeting that challenge, but not far. A common definition is that public interest means the 'welfare of the general public' or the 'common good'. Some definitions go on to distinguish what is otherwise implied, namely to differentiate public interest from individual self-interest or interests that are private, personal or parochial. Other definitional refinements are to distinguish between matters being 'of public interest' rather than 'of interest to the public', and between outcomes that are notionally of benefit to the community generally rather than of benefit only to a particular section or group. Those distinctions make sense and are undoubtedly what authors and speakers generally have in mind when they use the term. These popular or plain meaning definitions nevertheless mask layers of difficulty that cannot be ignored if the term is used to preference a particular viewpoint or outcome. Language can be troublesome when it is used to advance an unstated agenda.

The most obvious difficulty with using the term in a pluralist society is that it is problematic to make an uncontentious assertion as to the welfare of the common good on most major issues. Public policy choices frequently involve sharply conflicting claims. These conflicts have been apparent in recent public debates on budgetary priorities, energy policy, immigration detention, same-sex marriage and Constitutional disqualification from parliament. Defining the public interest in any of those areas is not straightforward although that does not impede the making of such claims.

There can also be both historical and cultural relativity in describing matters of public good or common interest. As one writer in *The Guardian* online noted:

> Fifty years ago it was assumed that there was a public interest in knowing that a parliamentarian was gay, but little or no public

interest in whether he drove home drunk, hit his wife or furnished his house using wood from non-sustainable sources. Now, obviously, it's the other way round.[3]

Technology is also now a vital element that complicates the task of ascertaining the common good, the public interest or community norms. Channels of communication between people are numerous and different to what they were even a decade ago. Digital channels create distinct communities who may interact very little with other communities. In former days it was more likely that people would receive news and information from the same sources – the print media, radio and nightly television news. The lines of debate and the main players were easily identifiable. Established government and community institutions played a central role in framing debate and forging a consensus on contested issues.

That situation has changed. Digital tools bring greater public engagement, but they also bring disruption, fragmentation and loss of community confidence in established institutions and processes. A Lowy Institute survey in 2008 revealed that only 49 per cent of Australians aged 18–29 years thought that democracy was the preferable form of government, compared to 77 per cent for those aged 60 years and over.[4] Similarly, the annual Gallup poll in the United States on 'Confidence in Institutions' shows that from 1985 to 2018 confidence in big business has fallen from 32 to 25 per cent, in newspapers from 35 to 23 per cent, in public schools from 48 to 29 per cent, in churches and organised religion from 66 to 38 per cent, in the Presidency from 52 to 37 per cent, in the Supreme Court from 56 to 37 per cent, and in Congress from 39 to 11 per cent.[5] As the Australian journalist Paul Kelly commented in relation to these trends, the fusion and interaction between new technology and culture has transformed democracy. He makes a number of important points.

> The earlier orthodoxy is that digital tools strengthen democracy by expanding voter engagement. This is true. But there are many

consequences. The Internet is the perfect anti-establishment tool; it is superb for single-issue campaigns; it is the ideal weapon to expose and depose governments. Since the Internet can challenge the established order, the pivotal question becomes: on whose behalf and in whose interest? What is happening to the national interest or public interest? It is not fanciful to suggest it is under attack or dying. This leads to a fundamental proposition. Does effective democracy actually require a range of intermediary institutions to set the context, promote debate and encourage a better-informed citizenry or is such thinking now hopelessly obsolete?[6]

One can only hope such institutions are not obsolete.

Fourth, and to draw these threads together, two clear themes emerge. The first theme is that public interest can be a somewhat vacuous concept if used loosely or indiscriminately. Lazy use of the term can polarise disagreement on an issue rather than capture agreement or commitment to a principled outcome. That is a self-defeating result if the purpose was to ascertain the common good. The second and contrasting theme is that the concept of public interest is resilient because of its intrinsic value. The wide use of the term in defining principles of law, leadership, governance and public service attests to this value. A commitment to public interest distils some of our most fundamental guiding principles. Among those principles I would prioritise the expectation that government should serve the people and not its own interests, that officials have an overarching obligation to differentiate between communal and self-interest, that the public interest and ethical behaviour are intertwined, and that transparent governance is essential to ensure that public interest principles are upheld. Those contrasting themes lay down a challenge. In the particular context in which the term is used, what is meant by public interest and how (or by who) is it ascertained? The process for clarifying the public interest is as important as the landing point.

I will illustrate my last observation by examining how the concept of public interest serves a valuable role in one area of law. I want to show its importance as a criterion that demarcates a crucial boundary between openness and confidentiality in government.

Public interest as a legal balancing test

Both in court proceedings and in handling access to information requests, there is a need to decide on occasions whether a particular document should be disclosed or remain confidential (or secret). In some instances the issue can be resolved by applying specific criteria – for example, the document is a trade secret, or disclosure would contravene a statutory secrecy provision. In other instances there are competing considerations, especially if the reason for non-disclosure is to protect the inner workings of government. In that situation the common law and freedom of information legislation employ a balancing test to produce an answer. All relevant considerations favouring non-disclosure are balanced against those favouring disclosure. The end result is that the public interest may favour either non-disclosure, or disclosure on an unconditional or conditional basis. Over time, to guide this balancing process a large number of public interest criteria have been identified by courts, tribunals and information commissioners. The body of legal principle and the legal processes for applying it are well understood and respected.

The balancing test story begins in 1978. In *Sankey v Whitlam*,[7] the High Court had to rule on a request for production of high level government documents that were sought in relation to a private prosecution brought by Sydney solicitor Danny Sankey against four Ministers in the Whitlam Labor Government (Gough Whitlam, Jim Cairns, Rex Connor and Lionel Murphy). Sankey alleged they had conspired to effect an unlawful purpose in pursuing a petro-dollar loan without properly going through the Loan Council approval process. The Fraser Coalition Government, which had no interest in defending or protecting the Labor Party, resisted production of the documents. Its resistance relied on the common law doctrine of Crown privilege which, at that time, held that a minister could issue a conclusive certificate to resist production of government documents for court proceedings.

In a landmark decision the High Court overturned the prevailing law and held that it is ultimately for a court to decide whether a claim of privilege will succeed. The court will rule on the privilege claim after balancing two aspects of the public interest: the public interest in safeguarding the efficient conduct of the affairs of government; and the public interest in ensuring that the administration of justice is not to be frustrated by the withholding of documents that may be essential if the substantive legal claim before the court is to succeed. The High Court held that this public interest balancing test would apply to all government documents and claims, including Cabinet documents and national security claims.

The doctrine of Crown Privilege considered in *Sankey v Whitlam* has since been reframed as the doctrine of public interest immunity. Over time an extensive case law has developed that spells out a range of public interest considerations that can be balanced one against another. Factors that may be relevant in a particular case include the age of the documents; their contents; the current sensitivity of issues dealt with in the documents; the degree of public knowledge of those issues; the purpose for which the documents are sought in the legal proceedings before the court; whether the contents of the documents may be central to the resolution of those proceedings; and whether there are special factors to consider such as Cabinet deliberations, commercial confidentiality or personal privacy. An oft-stated guiding principle is that 'The categories of public interest are not closed'.

The case law principles that have developed building on *Sankey v Whitlam* bear out a remark made in 1979 by the Senate Standing Committee on Legal and Constitutional Affairs in its report on freedom of information. The Committee supported the use of a public interest balancing test in the proposed *Freedom of Information (FOI) Act* and rejected the criticism that public interest was a nebulous or amorphous concept incapable of definition. The Committee said:

> [The] analysis by the [High] Court indicates that 'public interest' is a convenient and useful concept for aggregating any number of interests that may bear upon a disputed question that is of general – as opposed to merely private – concern. Although in that case the starting point was the nebulous interest of 'due administration of justice' and 'proper functioning of the public service', the Court broke these down to practical, recognisable considerations that were capable of being weighed – one against the other. The 'public interest' which has been described as an amorphous concept, incapable of useful definition, proved to be a viable concept enabling all relevant considerations to be brought to bear …
>
> In our view then, 'public interest' is a phrase that does not need to be, indeed could not usefully, be defined … Yet it is a useful concept because it provides a balancing test, by which any number of relevant interests may be weighed one against another.[8]

Notably, both the old and the new law were picked up in the FOI Act that commenced operation three years later in 1982. On the one hand, the Act included a public interest balancing test in exemptions that were designed to protect internal government processes relating to policy formulation, auditing and regulation. The Act also included, however, a mechanism for ministerial certificates that could conclusively decide that a document was exempt from disclosure for the reason that it was, for example, a Cabinet document or a policy document that should not be released on public interest grounds. The mechanism for conclusive certificates became the subject of regular criticism in the ensuing years and led to a High Court challenge in 2006 to test the grounds for issuing a certificate.[9] This culminated in two major reforms of the FOI Act. The first amendment in 2009 removed conclusive certificates from the Act. The second amendment in 2010 strengthened the public interest balancing test.[10]

The balancing test was enhanced in three ways. First, it was applied to a larger number of exemptions, including (in addition to policy processes) the exemptions protecting personal privacy, Commonwealth-State relations, business, the economy and research. Second, the test is weighted towards disclosure. Documents in the categories mentioned are described in the FOI Act as 'conditionally' exempt and must be released unless it would be contrary to the public interest to do so at the particular time.[11] Third, the Act spells out public interest factors that favour disclosure and identified factors that are irrelevant and cannot be considered.[12] Factors that favour disclosure and must be considered before an exemption decision is made include that disclosure could increase public participation in government processes, increase scrutiny and review of government activities, inform debate on matters of public importance, promote effective oversight of public expenditure, or enable individuals to access their own personal information. Irrelevant factors that cannot be considered in reaching an exemption decision are that disclosure could embarrass the government, could result in confusing or unnecessary debate, or that the document was authored at a high level in government.

The Office of the Australian Information Commissioner, which administers the FOI Act, has spelt out other public interest considerations in its guidelines and case decisions.[13] Below are two examples of situations in which the public interest balancing process is commonly undertaken. The first relates to the perennial issue of whether, from a public interest viewpoint, non-disclosure may be necessary to protect frankness and candour in internal deliberations. The Information Commissioner has been wary but not entirely dismissive of this claim. On the one hand, the view taken is that public servants have a duty to express their advice and opinions honestly and forthrightly. This duty is picked up in two of the APS Values mentioned in the *Public Service Act 1999* (section 10). The first, 'Accountable', is interpreted to mean 'the APS is open and accountable to the Australian community'. The second, 'Impartial', is interpreted to mean 'the APS is apolitical and provides the Government with advice that is frank, honest, timely and based on the best available evidence'. There is no hard evidence that Australia has created a supine and impoverished culture of public service after more than 35 years of FOI transparency.

On the other hand, the Information Commissioner has accepted that in particular circumstances candour could be diminished if it was known that a document being prepared for the government was likely to be released. If the diminution in candour would rob the document of its essential purpose, disclosure may be contrary to the public interest. An example is an incoming government brief written for an audience of one person – the new minister. It would lose its value if instead it were written as a document to be released publicly at the same time it was handed to the minister.[14] Another example is the comments that are voluntarily sent by company auditors to ASIC to alert it to potential probity issues but might not be sent if the auditors encountered hostility from companies that became aware they were the subject of alert notices.[15]

A second illustration of the public interest balancing test being applied is in relation to the disclosure of documents containing the names of public servants. Government agencies persistently attempted to redact the names of non-Senior Executive Service Officers from non-exempt documents. The Information Commissioner consistently rebuffed this practice, ruling that it was arbitrary and artificial. Public servants names must be left in documents unless there is some special reason for non-disclosure, such as a person's fear of physical danger through being identified in a document.[16] On the other hand, the Commissioner has also been more tolerant of allowing officials to redact their telephone numbers and signatures, and to remove names of junior staff from documents that are published on the web under the Disclosure Log.[17]

Concluding thoughts

The whole concept of the public interest is necessarily imprecise. It depends upon context and is unavoidably open textured. When used loosely or indiscriminately in public discourse it achieves little other than to suggest that the speaker is either skating over the need for more refined analysis of a multi-faceted issue or is using the concept to mask a contestable assertion or faltering argument. Used sparingly and adeptly, public interest can be a valuable concept. Many legal doctrines certainly rely upon the public interest for their cogency. Public interest can also be the most convenient concept we have available for inviting consideration of, and then balancing, competing considerations that are relevant to a problem that requires a legal answer or a practical response. Used in that way, the concept of public interest can describe both the process of reasoning and the conclusion. It would be difficult to know how public administration and political debate could be conducted without it.

Endnotes

1. *Report of the Royal Commission into Commercial Activities of Government and Other Matters* (1992), Section 3.2.
2. Jane Johnston, 'Whose interests? Why defining the "public interest" is such a challenge', *The Conversation*, 24 Sept 2017.
3. Online comment quoted in Johnston.
4. Lowy Institute Poll 2018, 'Understanding Australian attitudes to the world'.
5. <www.gallup.com> The 'Confidence' figure is the combined 'Great deal/quite a lot' responses. The earlier Presidency figure is from 1975.
6. Paul Kelly, 'West challenged in a spinning world', *The Australian*, 23 December 2017.
7. (1978) 142 CLR 1.
8. Senate Standing Committee on Constitutional and Legal Affairs, *Freedom of Information*, Report (1979) paras 5.25, 5.28.
9. *McKinnon v Secretary, Department of the Treasury* (2006) 228 CLR 423.

10 The changes are outlined in Office of the Australian Information Commissioner, *Guide to the Freedom of Information Act 1982* (2011) Ch 2.
11 *Freedom of Information Act 1982* Pt IV, Div 3.
12 *Freedom of Information Act 1982* s 11B.
13 See *Guidelines issued by the Australian Information Commissioner under s 93A of the Freedom of Information Act 1982*, Part 6.
14 *Crowe and Department of the Treasury* [2013] AICmr 69.
15 *Cornerstone Legal Pty Ltd and Australian Securities and Investments Commission* [2013] AICmr 71.
16 See OAIC *Guidelines* at paras 6.1.52–57.
17 See OAIC *Guidelines* at para 14.19.

CHAPTER 2

The public interest and the common good: synonymous or subset?

Andrew Cameron

This chapter considers the public interest from the perspective of the 'common good' to test whether these terms are synonymous; and if not, to delineate how notions of the common good might illuminate our understanding of the public interest. To that end, we need also to consider what is meant by 'common good' and whether it is useful as a theoretical construct. This task might seem a preliminary one but it actually provides the bulk of my contribution to the subject.

In a straw poll of half a dozen texts in political theory and public policy, several with special reference to Australia, there is little specification of the 'public interest' and even less of the 'common good'. Just as this collection of essays is predicated on the observation that the 'public interest' is somehow self-evident, the 'common good' is similarly used without specification and just as frequently. Furthermore, each term can be used to define the other. In the *Oxford Companion to Australian Politics*, 'the public good, "common good" or "public interest" as it is often called, concerns what is in the best interests of the society as a whole rather than what is good for individuals'.[1] This equation looks simple enough. If 'public interest' is synonymous with 'common good' then all a public officer would need to do their job is a straightforward depiction of common good. But that depiction is not so simple, and the equation of the common good with the public interest may not be so simple if the 'common good' is a term without definite meaning or agreed content.

To get at this 'common good', I will 'pan the camera back' and indulge in a little etymology, philosophy, history and theology. First, I will consider what the founders had in mind when they proposed establishing the 'Commonwealth' of Australia during the 1890s. Second, I will draw on philosophical and economic analyses of the common good to clarify its relationship to public interest. Third, I will conclude with some practical suggestions for public officers keen to have some conceptual definitions they can work with. I readily concede that their daily engagement with people and problems make them much more qualified than I to determine the best practical steps to take. My modest aim is to clarify some of the complexity and to suggest why some matters of public deliberation have proven to be difficult.

In brief, I contend that the public's interest is in the common good; that actions initiated in the public interest describe the execution of judgments that either advance common good or maintain cultural space for the common good to be pursued; that the common good has many facets, some that precede and outlast particular societies, others that constitute a society in its own particular time and place; that the term 'public interest', like the term 'common good', is complex and contested but not hopelessly so; and, therefore, as representative moral agents, public officers do well to articulate what is contested, where there is consensus, and how their own estimates of common good can guide actions and direct policies toward the public interest.

My interest in theology has some bearing on the topic and its treatment. Why? Because much in the Western liberal order would not have happened without the insights of Christian theology. But in a discussion of the common good, it would be problematic if anyone felt religiously 'got-at' by the inclusion of this consideration. Furthermore, I readily concede that the notion of common good has coalesced from various sources. Even so, I will include some aspects of Christian thought of benefit to all.

A 'Commonwealth'

For Australians, an elementary historical point illuminates our present experience, whether or not we judge it to be determinative of our future. Simply put, upholding the public interest reflects a shared effort to govern a 'Commonwealth' where a 'Commonwealth' reflects 'common weal'. 'Weal' is an archaic word for 'good', so 'common wealth' was never primarily about a 'wealth' of money held in common. 'Wealth' once referred to how much 'weal' one enjoyed. Only later did it refer to a portfolio of possessions.

The *Oxford English Dictionary* lists the varied use of this compound noun from the fifteenth century. In 1871, the great English social critic John Ruskin contrasts 'striving for a Common-Wealth or for a Common-Illth'. Here the concept of a society based on shared collective good is opposed to the prospect of a society where all decline together. This concept of shared good comes by way of synecdoche to refer to all who share it: 'a whole body of people, the body politic; a state, community'.[2] The two senses come together when the commons plead with King Henry VIII that he leave his successor 'a Commune Weale to governe, and not an iland of brute beastes, among who the strongest devour the weaker'.[3]

Given this long history there is no simple way to pin down the word or any value in attempting to be stipulative. Defining 'common good' does not make it so. Nor can some formalist assertion of a common good by the founders of the Australian Commonwealth ensure its political validity today. The Australian historian Sir Keith Hancock notes that in sixteenth century England the term was appropriated and contested by idealists, reactionaries, realists, rebels and special interests, each of whom had mutually exclusive accounts of the goods worth sharing and how to share them.[4] The same is true today. Even so, our founders' *prima facie* appeal to a 'Commonwealth' set the conditions under which we now operate and shaped some of what we assume. A fair degree of deliberation went into naming Australia a Commonwealth, and degree of literacy attended their use of the term.

The Australian historian JA La Nauze has shown how the 'Father of Federation', Sir Henry Parkes, was 'socialising' the term from the 1880s.[5] It was ardently championed by the liberal politician Alfred Deakin during the years spanning the constitutional conventions and finally brought across the line by Edmund Barton, the new nation's first prime minister. A 2,000 octavo-page treatise by the Scottish jurist Viscount James Bryce, *The American Commonwealth*, had been published in 1888 and was well-known among convention delegates.[6] Bryce makes ample reference in his text to the United States as a 'commonwealth' of sorts, yet offers no in-principle definition of a 'commonwealth' since his intention was to 'paint the institutions and the people of America as they are' independent of any political theory, philosophical origin or historical development.[7] Bryce's matter-of-fact use of the term suggests that by 1888 it was linguistic common-coin for a shared cultural concept.

The substantial 'thickness' of the concept in the Australian context becomes evident when it survived a final challenge in the convention debate of 1897 when the delegates bickered about the new nation's name. Some argued for 'United Australia', and others for 'Australasia' given that in time it would probably encompass New Zealand and Fiji. But the main substantive objection to 'commonwealth' was that it had overtones of anti-monarchical sentiment since Oliver Cromwell styled the English Protectorate of 1649–60 (essentially a republic) a 'Commonwealth'. Barton finally shut down that connotation by supplanting it with explicit reference to our 'common weal':

> Commonwealth is the greatest and most stately name by which a great association of self-governing people can be characterised. I have no objection to the name, although at one time or another the name has been got hold of and misused. Modern English

writers are now accustomed to allude to a certain period as the Protectorate, and not as the Commonwealth. We are entitled to take this word 'Commonwealth,' because in all the attributes of a self-governing country for the common weal this Constitution will be in its main provisions completed and made perfect.[8]

At the same time, people like the English liberal Sir Henry Campbell-Bannerman were advocating for a 'British Commonwealth' rather than an 'Empire'. The story is told of an after-dinner speech in 1900 where Campbell-Bannerman hosted Australian visitors. A reporter recounted his speech:

> The proverb ran that there was no rose without a thorn, and there was one thorn in the rose offered by their honoured guests. It lay in the title of 'Australian Commonwealth'. Where could they find a word more exactly indicating the intent and purpose of that great aggregated community of which we were all proud to be citizens, and which included all the dominions of Her Majesty? In that great creation of the energy of our people in the past and in the present we sought only the welfare and prosperity of all and to make the common weal shared by all for the use of all. That was the ideal of our Australian friends, and how could it be better expressed than by the homely native phrase the British Commonwealth? But we had been too late. These enterprising kinsmen of ours from the other end of the world had appropriated the word, and he confessed he owed them a grudge for it.[9]

So 'common weal' was integral to shared conceptions of a Commonwealth, and by extension, integral to their conception of what the Australian Constitution was designed to uphold. But as Hancock put it:

> Our nation has always excelled in political artistry rather than in political science, and the artist's skill can never be reduced to formulae. Our principle of the commonwealth is an English secret,

whose clue is maintained in the whole of English history. The name commonwealth is like a cave recessed in endless passages and grottoes; and in each grotto there is an echo. Australia has added to those echoes.[10]

The point of starting with the name of our nation is not to stipulate a meaning or to coerce a consensus through historical warrant. But we can certainly say from history that we cannot make our 'public interest habit' intelligible without some awareness of these origins.

'Common Good' in theology, philosophy and economics

Any conception of 'common good' is premised on the notion that something good is out there; or to borrow from ancient Greek philosophical tradition, that we move among many 'goods' (where 'goods' meant much more than objects we buy). To demonstrate the point, I invite the reader to pause for fifteen seconds and to note down or imagine whatever good things you think we all share.

The question is deliberately wide-open, and many disparate candidates will emerge. The panoply of options at least includes: shared resources, such as land, water, ore, and fisheries; shared values, such as for 'personal autonomy' or 'tolerance'; shared cultural space, as we manoeuvre around each other in quests for individual and/or familial fulfilment; shared justice, as we pursue 'equity' in material or information distribution, bureaucratic procedures, civil redress or criminal punishment; some shared 'essence', such as a flourishing of relationships, or the maximisation of harmonious multicultural diversity; some shared 'destiny', such as protection of national sovereignty or maximisation of national interests, 'we can even curb our shared weakness' in common, as when a declaration of conflict of interest curbs human greed; or a 'sin tax' dis-incentivises addiction to alcohol, cigarettes, or gambling; or a 'public health initiative' moralises against predilections to domestic violence, sexual harassment, speeding, or driving under the influence.

This plethora of 'goods' is hard to encompass. Depending on the angle of view, some of them may cohere in a consistent entity. Curbing shared weaknesses might, for example, assist human flourishing through enhanced relationships. Others on the list may not seem commensurate: pursuits of equity clash notoriously with some accounts of individual fulfilment and expressions of personal autonomy.

A long history of Judeo-Christian reflection on this plethora is nonetheless optimistic about the essential goodness of what surrounds us. In the Bible, God invents then declares everything 'very good' (Genesis 1:24); God is the source of 'every generous act of giving, with every perfect gift', according to Jesus' brother (James 1:17); 'everything created by God is good, and nothing is to be rejected' according to the apostle Paul (1 Timothy 4:4). This optimism found powerful agreement with Greek philosophical emphases that we encounter in Neoplatonism. For the fourth-century African theologian Augustine of Hippo, who was influenced both by the Bible and Neoplatonism, it is as if there is so much good 'out there' that no one person can see it all at once. Our sins therefore consist, in the first instance, in missing or underrating things that should matter to us; and, in the second instance, in ruining human relationships by converting the pursuit of each good into a perception of scarcity prompting fights to secure them.

Augustine went on to assert that every society is, in part, constituted by its 'common objects of love'. By this he meant those goods for which so many people have an affection that we coalesce into whole societies constituted by common cause to acquire these objects of collective 'love'.[11] The long history of theological reflection on the common good that followed this insight culminated in a body of thought known as Catholic Social Teaching. I will consider these ideas through the work of one thinker within that tradition, the Capuchin Brother and medical doctor Daniel Sulmasy.

Noticing that 'the term "common good" has a lot of different kinds of meanings',[12] Sulmasy offers a typology of the various uses of the term. His contribution has become a touchstone for sorting out conceptual confusion. (I need to mention his own acknowledgement that his account is premised on a well-defined social unit. Just as Federation acknowledged that Australia would be comprised of smaller social units, political theory has also discussed the relative primacies of various social units, such as when Catholic Social Teaching advocates for the dignity and authority of smaller social units in its doctrine of 'subsidiarity'.) Sulmasy's 'four basic notions' form their own subdivisions. Table 1 is my summary of his account.

Table 1: Sulmasy's typology of the usages of the term 'common good'

1. *The aggregative common good* is the overall sum of the goods of all the individuals in a social unit.
    a. In its early *sentimentalist* form it is whatever delivers 'the greatest good for the greatest number', irrespective of how 'bads' are distributed.
    b. In its later *utilitarian* form it is the net of satisfied preferences after 'bads' are subtracted.
2. *The common common good* denotes the goods that each member of the social unit relies upon.
    a. Its *possessive* usage refers to natural entities held in common, such as land, air, water and public spaces.
    b. Its *teleological* usage refers to our inclinations to basic common forms of human flourishing, such as friendship, happiness, or spiritual truth.
3. *The supersessive common good* refers to claims to goods believed to be above all the individuals who constitute the community.
    a. In its *factional* form, it refers to whatever pleases those who control the State.
    b. In its *Hegelian* form, it refers to the shared social norms and values of the community that are believed to be synthesised and represented by the State.

4. *The integral common good* is a kind of good arising explicitly from mutual human interaction, which cannot be further subdivided.

   a. Its *conditional* form refers to the parameters we must share to enable each individual to flourish – for example, the agreed practice of tolerance or non-maleficence.

   b. Its *constitutive* form refers to the community of relationships with other human beings from which no one can ever truly abstract themselves, so that elemental to 'my' good is the good of the others with whom I regularly engage.

Economists Tim Murphy and Jeff Parkey have applied economic analysis to Sulmasy's taxonomy of usage.[13] In order to understand their conclusions I need to explain their analytical terminology. These terms are outlined in Table 2. They produce a species of good in each quadrant of the table, denoted respectively as 'private', 'common', 'club' or 'toll', and 'public' goods. These terms arise from the parameters used on each axis of the table: 'excludable' and 'non-excludable', 'rivalrous' and 'non-rivalrous'.

For the economist, a 'good' of any kind is something that provides satisfaction to its user. These are then susceptible to 'excludability' and 'rivalry'. You and I are 'excluded' from a good if we cannot or will not bear a burden for its benefits. Most of us are excluded from, say, owning a Bugatti Veyron Grand Sport Vitesse supercar, which requires a down-payment on order of $US350,000. Conversely a fireworks display is available to all making it non-excludable. A good is 'rivalrous' when consumption of it depletes its stock. At the time of writing, all models of Bugatti Veyron were completely sold out. Conversely, parklands in Canberra are currently non-rivalrous as these parks will take some years to be utilised to capacity.

Table 2: Terms use for analysis of economic goods[14]

	Excludable	Non-excludable
Rivalrous	*Private goods*, such as: housing food clothing supercars	*Common goods*, such as: fisheries beaches over-utilised parks
Non-rivalrous	*Club (or Toll) goods*, such as: toll roads Netflix	*Public goods*, such as: national defence environmental protection lighthouses fireworks displays under-utilised parks

The terms in Table 2 are only the standard professional tools used in Murphy's and Parkey's discipline to analyse tangible goods, such as the examples in the table. What is of interest for our purposes is their mapping of Sulmasy's taxonomy to this table, especially given that Sulmasy's categories mostly refer to more abstract and intangible 'goods'. Table 3 summarises their conclusions:

Table 3: Sulmasy's categories of common good terms mapped to economic terms of analysis

	Excludable	Non-excludable
Rivalrous	*Private goods*	*Common goods* possessive common
Non-rivalrous	*Club (or Toll) goods* utilitarian aggregative factional supersessive Hegelian supersessive	*Public goods* sentimentalist aggregative teleological common conditional integral constitutive integral

I believe it unnecessary to repeat the arguments of Murphy and Parkey in detail because Table 3 already delivers sufficient clarity about what is in the public interest. I will suggest how this is so using the labels attached to each quadrant.

In our polity, we all agree that *private* goods are not common goods, and that organised sharing of them occurs through the market. The establishment, maintenance and regulation of a stable market is a matter of public interest and what goods should migrate to market-based supply (become 'privatised') is obviously a discussion of public interest. Even so, this quadrant in Table 3 is blank for good reason. It represents general agreement (in a neo-liberal polity, at least) that private markets are a domain requiring a degree of non-intervention by public officers. In the top right quadrant of Tables 2 and 3, the proliferation of the term *common* is annoying and imprecise. Nevertheless, we all agree that the rivalrous and excludable 'common (possessive) common goods' on view should be available to all. Furthermore, it is in the public interest to regulate shared access to these goods. Proposals to abdicate such regulation by their migration to become 'private' goods are highly contested discussions of public interest although government carriage of their regulation (for example, through various forms of licensing) can perhaps be regarded as the most straightforward expression of government of the common good for the public interest.

The *public* goods of the bottom right quadrant are such high-level abstractions as to make it almost unintelligible to imagine how government in the public interest might relate to them. These are the stuff of our most cosmic anthropological claims. As such, they are beyond the competence of any branch of government to arbitrate. The extent to which our common good is integrally constituted by the quality of our relationships or integrally conditioned by our individual freedom to participate in cultural space, this is the stuff of philosophical and religious reflection. Such cultural reflection will undoubtedly influence the intuitions and 'wisdom' of government actors. But what constitutes the public interest here can never be settled. Perhaps the best that can be said (within a liberal polity) is that the public interest is best served by maintaining ample freedom for civil society to ponder, discuss, research and reflect upon the nature of these intangible public goods.

Table 3 is most interesting and controversial in its conclusions about club or toll goods. As Murphy and Parkey put it, '[t]hrough this analysis we show that in several cases philosophical conceptions of the common good are not "common" at all, at least not in the general and shared way one expects of a viable conceptualization of the common good.'[15] That assessment is most obviously the case for factional supersessive common goods that are basically special interest claims posing as common goods. These are easily seen in cases of corruption where someone rules in the interest of self, family or club while claiming to do so 'for the common good'.

Far more controversial in our context are Murphy's and Parkey's consignments of utilitarian aggregative and Hegelian supersessive common goods to club goods. To improvise upon their theme: an 'Australian value' (already a surreptitious common good claim), such as 'tolerance' is a candidate for an Hegelian supersessive common good, since the state embodies and enforces a perceived community commitment to this virtue. Also, a bureaucratic commitment to maximising satisfied preferences presumes the supremacy of a procedural approach to common good against other approaches. In both cases, a particular conception of common good – which arguably reflects the agreements of some 'club' or 'elite' – rules us all.

The German political theorist Clause Offe pointedly illustrates what has happened now that Western liberal bureaucracies squarely inhabit and uphold both utilitarian and Hegelian supersessive accounts of the common good. Since politico-legal order and the success of various policies rely upon sympathetic support by citizens with compatible dispositions, political elites respond with:

> a polyphonous chorus of targeted bureaucratic ads for virtue that go far beyond 'moral suasion' … Citizens thus see themselves

confronted at every turn today by quasi-educational appeals that ask them, for example, to bring children into the world and raise them with care; to exercise consideration and caution in traffic; to sort household trash and make other sacrifices for ecological reasons; to practise safer sex; to avoid criminal offences and to cooperate in police investigations; to maintain their health through preventive measures of correct diet and abstinence; to observe standards of cleanliness in public, as when taking the dog for a walk; to pay their taxes conscientiously and treat members of other cultures and ethnic groups with respect. It would be good to know more about the methods and success of this multifaceted program of training in virtue, officially instituted and interfaced with common-good arguments. Here a conjecture must suffice: that the agents of government policy are aware that they cannot manage with their own instruments – legislation, executive and judicial enforcement, and fiscal incentives – and thus depend on the norms and disciplinary effects of the citizens' public spirit.[16]

The average public servant in Australia will no doubt recognise that he or she is one among legions involved in such indoctrination. But is it in 'the public interest'? My answer is that it is sufficient simply to observe that the question cannot actually be answered, philosophically speaking, if the 'common goods' ostensibly being served are actually 'club goods' masquerading as common. If the public servant has a sense of unease at being involved in this kind of public education, it may be due to inadequate reflection and deliberation, 'upstream' of these policies, about the nature of political society as such.

Proposals for acting in the public interest toward the common good

The unnerving questions residing within the club goods quadrant of Table 3 may seem depressingly insurmountable. Although the intersection of public interest and common good are the most complex here, the complexity of Table 3 also shows that public interest judgments for responsible government are made by living, breathing morals agents within contexts kaleidoscopic with goods that are worth their continuing attention and deliberation. That alone is sufficient reason to persist. Some parameters for a judgment made 'in the public interest' can now be offered. Complaints, such as those of Offe, may only indicate that action in the public interest have become 'over-responsible government' at some points.

First, executive government's action in the public interest is directly concerned with identifying and upholding access to non-excludable goods and indirectly concerned with setting the conditions for excludable goods to be shared privately. Respect for the market as the domain of private goods exchange is logically complemented by public interest discussions and judgments about the extent of market self-regulation, and the norms of privatisation.

Second, thoughtful public officers can discern and unmask any factional 'club good' masquerading as common good.

Third, for the tangible goods of Table 2, public officers are certainly called upon to handle those non-excludable goods that are migrating from non-rivalrous to rivalrous because it is definitely in the public interest to arbitrate orderly access to such shared non-excludable goods.

Fourth, for the intangible public goods of Table 3, public officers do well to uphold the 'freedom' of the public to reflect upon and weigh these matters and inhabit them as they see fit. Simultaneously, public officers can guard against the chilling effect upon such reflection that occurs when someone's accounts of conditional, constitutive or teleological common good illicitly migrates to become a supersessive Hegelian good, or (and this is more difficult to keep in check) when some aggregative utilitarian procedure comes to dominate as the only kind of common good. In other words, public officers should have a say in preventing government from promoting these club goods as common goods, should they believe that is occurring.

Unfortunately, a tangent related to the politics of identity must also be observed. Canadian political philosophers Jonah Goldstein and

Jeremy Rayner argue that identity claims are fundamentally different from interest claims. Indeed, identity claims are deeply incommensurate. Because 'interests' in all their forms often involve things external to us, 'the negotiating process itself often serves to clarify those interests'; whereas identity disputes often include claimants who 'resist clarifying what they really want, even to themselves' so that 'no matter what I get (what interests are satisfied), I may continue to wonder if what I get really recognises who I am'.[17] This side-note draws our attention to a matter that cannot be simplified in the modern situation and is the reason why endless disputes pivoting upon identity may remain despite the public officer's best efforts to clarify interests and goods in the field.

Conclusion

The common good is complex and contested. We need not despair, however, that the common good does not exist. Christian thought contends that we are upheld by the gift of inhabitation within an essentially good cosmos that no human folly can ever finally overturn. Even for those who do not accept that view, the burden of proof remains on anyone who wishes to persuade us that there is no common weal in Australia – not only because of our Constitution but because we will always share things and need each other.

Something can be philosophically 'vague' – that is, hard to find boundaries for – yet still be real and worth the effort to define and explore. Mount Everest, love and friendship are all 'vague' in that way: we don't precisely know where they start and stop. The same can be said of the common good and possibly the public interest as well. But 'vague' does not entail a 'taboo'. The vagueness of public interest and common good as concepts should not be allowed to degenerate into taboo. In other words a clear and present danger for our polity is that the public interest may become a 'taboo' practice in the sense outlined by the philosopher Alisdair McIntyre. When Cook's men asked Polynesian islanders why men and women in that culture ate separately, the only answer that could be given was that it is 'taboo'; no further rationale could be found. As a result, the practice quickly died out.[18] Similarly, without the rational intelligibility fostered by continuing attempts at articulation – grounded, I suggest, in substantive accounts of the common weal of this Commonwealth – acting in the 'public interest' risks becoming something we only do because it is 'taboo'. Such an attitude will ensure it simply goes away.

Therefore serious analysis and reflection along the lines introduced here might offer a framework from within which a public officer can say, 'I have determined that action X is in the public interest because it upholds and advances this set 'A' of goods we share, does no damage this set 'B' of goods we share, and/or does not permit sectional interests illicitly to colonise our common concerns.' We might not agree with this judgement. But a public interest judgment needs at least to be defensible in more terms than mere appeal to the phrase itself. With no intelligibility attached to some kind of substantive evaluation of what is good, the public suspects a club-good masquerading as the common good. Worse is the prospect that citizens suspect that the public officer speaks only from an empty taboo. Conversely, enough public statements along these lines might rebuild the public's damaged trust in the polity's decision-makers. It's certainly worth the effort.

Endnotes

1. J Moss, 'Public Good', in *The Oxford Companion to Australian Politics*, edited by B Galligan and W Roberts, Oxford University Press, 2007, p. 471.
2. *Oxford English Dictionary*, Second Edition on CD-ROM (v. 4.0.0.3), Oxford University Press, 2009, *s.v.* 'commonwealth' and 'common-weal'.
3. Cited in WK Hancock, 'A Veray and True Comyn Wele', in *Politics in Pitcairn and Other Essays*, MacMillan & Co. Ltd, 1947 [1932], p. 101.
4. Hancock 1947 [1932], p. 103.
5. JA La Nauze, 'The name of the Commonwealth of Australia', *Historical Studies*, vol. 15, no. 57, 1971, pp. 62–68.
6. Historian JSF Wright gives an expansive account of Bryce's influence on the Conventions' practical reasoning through Bryce's representation of U.S. federal institutions 'as essentially English institutions adapted to American circumstances': JSF Wright, 'Anglicizing the United States Constitution: James Bryce's Contribution to Australian Federalism', *Publius: The Journal of Federalism*, vol. 31, no. 4, 2001, p. 107.
7. Wright 2001, p. 109, quoting Bryce.
8. National Australasian Convention, *Official report of the National Australasian Convention debates, Adelaide, 1897, South Australia*, C E Bristow, Government Printer, p. 618.
9. Cited in SR Mehrotra, 'On the use of the term "commonwealth"', *Journal of Commonwealth Political Studies*, vol. 2, no. 1, 1963, p. 9.
10. Hancock 1947 [1932], p. 98.
11. This concept is more fully explored by the UK Anglican political theologian OMT O'Donovan, *Common Objects of Love: Moral Reflection and the Shaping of Community*, Eerdmans, 2002.
12. DP Sulmasy, 'Four basic notions of the common good', *St. John's Law Review*, vol. 75, no. 2, 2001, p. 303.
13. T Murphy and J Parkey, 'An economic analysis of the philosophical common good', *International Journal of Social Economics*, vol. 43, no. 8, 2016, pp. 823–40.
14. Modelled on Murphy and Parkey 2016, p. 826, Table I.
15. Murphy and Parkey 2016, p. 826.
16. C Offe, 'Whose good is the common good?', *Philosophy & Social Criticism*, vol. 38, no. 7, 2012, p. 669.
17. J Goldstein and J Rayner, 'The politics of identity in late modern society', *Theory and Society*, vol. 23, no. 3, 1994, p. 367.
18. A MacIntyre, *After Virtue: A Study in Moral Theory*, Third edition, University of Notre Dame Press, 2007, p. 111.

CHAPTER 3

The public interest: ensuring good public administration and accountability

Chris Wheeler

The overarching obligation on public officials is to act in the public interest. The verb act implies all aspects of official conduct and encompasses protecting and promoting the public interest from threats and indifference. Acting in the public interest is fundamental to the preservation of a representative democratic system of government and the practice of good public administration. To use the state of New South Wales as an example, there are references to the 'public interest' in over 250 separate pieces of legislation and over 50 regulations. From my experience of the past thirty years working in government compliance and oversight, there are at least three major obstacles to public officials acting in the public interest.

First, public interest is one of the most used terms in the context of public administration but it is arguably the least defined and least understood. I have asked many public officials to explain what the term means and to outline its ramifications in practice. Few have any clear idea and this is worrying when the public interest is meant to be the cornerstone of their conduct. Second, identifying or determining the relevant public interest is often difficult when dealing with complex matters involving a number of stakeholders. The complexity is exacerbated by the conflicts that can arise between the obligations on public officials to serve the parliament, to serve the incumbent government (that is, the ruling political party or coalition), to serve the agency that actually employs them, and to serve the public as consumers of the things governments provide. Third, there is more to acting in the public interest than doing the right thing once you have identified what the right thing is. This is only partly correct. In practice, it can be very difficult to do the right thing where the consequences are likely to be unwelcome. For instance, arguing with senior managers or political masters comes at a personal and sometimes professional cost. Despite these difficulties, the starting point must remain the same: government officials, institutions and agencies are obliged to act in the public interest.[1] Advancing this principle must come first. Dealing with practical complexities is a second order matter.

Defining the 'public interest'

I have long contended that the public interest is best seen as the objective of, or the approach to be adopted in, decision-making rather than as a specific and immutable outcome that can be achieved.[2] The foremost intention is directing consideration and action away from private, personal, parochial or partisan interests towards broader, by which is meant more 'public', interests. This is the critical concept that needs to be observed when the term is applied in different contexts. Applying the term is a separate issue because descriptions of the public interest will vary depending on the particular circumstances in which the term is used although the concept remains the same. For instance, decisions about whether to close a government school will be based on very different considerations than decisions relating to the allocation of water resources but the need for public officials to be mindful of the broader interests is the same.

On several occasions the Courts have tried to offer guidance on what the concept might mean in a legal context. These attempts have been of minimal practical assistance to public officials.[3] More beneficial would be a reasonably simple definition or conceptual statement that outlines, in general terms, what the 'public interest' means or the concerns that it addresses. I have seen the public interest variously described as: the sum of special interests or of all private interests; the net result of individuals pursuing their self interest; the broad shared interests of society; the shared/collective goals or values of the community (on which there is consensus); the views, interests or will of the majority; and the public good or the common good.

These definitions are unsatisfying. They are either too vague or too broad so as to include practically anything and everything or so specific and technical that they require sensitive measurements to determine their presence. My main dissatisfaction is that none of them clearly address circumstances where an individual's private interests – for example in the right to silence, privacy and procedural fairness – are in the 'public interest'. In other words, where the collective interest of a society is best served by something that is experienced on an individual basis. A society that denies individuals the right to privacy is one encouraging the development of a highly intrusive state that eventually will turn on its own citizens. In some circumstances each of these rights has a downside whether relating to cost, greater difficulty in identify and proving wrongdoing, and so on. But the protection of these rights is considered to be in the public interest because they are the shared rights of all citizens. Plainly, important public interests can conflict at times.

Furthermore, many descriptions encompass the notion that meeting the particular needs or addressing the special interests of a sub-set of the public may well be in the public interest though doing so will not directly benefit, or may indeed in some ways actually compete with the interests of, the larger public. Governments often provide special support funding to groups with special needs at the expense of those without these needs. The objective of such funding is sometimes to prevent any group within society feeling they are unwanted or without worth. An example is funding educational and rehabilitation programs for the incarcerated. These individuals were sentenced to prison as punishment for their crimes but governments provide taxpayer funding to minimise the likelihood of them reoffending when released back into the community. Educating and training prisoners at public expense diverts funding from other community needs but is deemed to be in the public interest if the outcome is a society in which persons and property are more safe and secure. The public interest in this situation needs to be considered in terms of broader benefits to the public. The amounts invested will always be the subject of comment; the application of the investment must always reflect the public interest.

An overriding shared commitment within a society is the importance placed on fairness. This commitment includes addressing the particular needs of disadvantaged or vulnerable individuals and groups. For example, this can involve actions to: preserve social harmony (fairness in terms of equity); adequately distribute resources (fairness in terms of equality); or, otherwise foster the welfare of disadvantaged individuals or groups (fairness in terms of needs). There is, then, one description in the list of possibilities I mentioned earlier that could be an acceptable short description. The public interest is concerned with 'the common good'. This description encompasses the protection of the rights and interests of individuals while addressing the particular needs or interests of sub-groups of the community. Aligning the public interest with the common good certainly points us in the right direction.

Key social norms

We need to be clear about what working 'in' the public interest looks like because it is the basis for a number of key societal norms that shape public sector conduct and guide official decision-making. The key societal norms that should guide people exercising public official functions or acting in a public official capacity reflect three distinct impulses. The first is, of course, the concept of the public interest. The second is ethics. There is an absolute obligation on public officials to act ethically in the performance of their official functions. Third is administrative law. Public sector officials and agencies are legally obliged to comply with the principles and rules of administrative law, which are intended to protect the rights of the public and to ensure that government power is exercised appropriately.

These three key sources essentially address the same issues but they vary in approach. The public interest issues focus on guiding consideration as to what is in the best interests of the community, the 'common good'. The ethical obligations focus on considerations as to what is morally right or wrong. Administrative law principles and rules focus on considerations as to what is legal, fair and reasonable. I have argued that while most discussion about the public interest focuses on the merits of decisions and on outcomes, public officials are required to be mindful of four considerations when acting in the public interest. They must consider *outcomes* – the merits of decisions and actions. They must consider *inputs* – what the decision maker considers when making a decision. They must consider *process* – acting in accordance with legal requirements, acting impartially and apolitically, acting fairly, reasonably and with proportionality while being accountable and transparent. They must consider *conduct* – they should act in good faith, be unbiased and respectful.

The application of the other key societal norms that guide people exercising public official functions or acting in a public official capacity (ethical obligations, administrative law principles and rules) have similar dimensions. The requirement on public officials to act ethically means they must consider:

outcomes-decisions – acting fairly and in the public interest;

inputs – acting legally, honestly, for the proper purpose, within power and impartially; avoiding bias, only considering relevant matters; and managing conflicts of interests;

procedures-processes – acting fairly, including providing procedural fairness; and ensuring no improper delay, and

conduct-approach – acting honestly and in the public interest; providing procedural fairness; appropriately protecting privacy; giving reasons for decisions; and giving frank and candid advice.

The requirement on public officials to observe administrative law principles and rules means they must consider:

outcomes-decisions – acting within power fairly and in the public interest;

inputs – acting legally, honestly, for the proper purpose, within power and impartially; avoiding bias; only considering relevant matters; and managing conflicts of interests, procedural fairness (the evidence and bias rules);

procedures-processes – acting fairly, including providing procedural fairness (the hearing rule) and avoiding unreasonable delay; and

conduct-approach – acting honestly and in the public interest by providing procedural fairness (for example the notice rule), protecting privacy, explaining decisions and giving frank and candid advice.

Practical benefits

There are obvious practical benefits flowing from public officials adhering to these societal norms and conducting themselves in accordance with the high standards expected by the public. Unfavourable decisions are more likely to be tolerated by the people who are affected by them if they perceive that the decision-maker has met generally accepted standards of conduct and decision-making.

Organisational scientists have devised 'organisational justice theory' or 'justice theory' as a way to describe and explain how individuals react to decisions and the way they are made. Forty years ago, two social scientists contended that disputants care as much about how their disputes are resolved as they do about the outcomes they receive.[4] Research into 'justice theory' has shown that where the people affected by a decision perceive that the procedures followed to reach that decision and the way they were treated were fair, they are far more likely to accept an unfavourable outcome or decision as fair and reasonable in the circumstances.[5] In other words, people are more likely to accept decisions or outcomes that they see as unfavourable to them if they believe those decisions or outcomes arose out of a fair process in which they were treated with respect and given adequate information.

Organisational scientists suggest there are three dimensions of any decision-making process, that encompass the four considerations I referred to earlier:

> *outcomes/decisions* of the process (referred to as *distributive justice*) focussing on the perceived fairness of decisions or outcomes of the process;
>
> *procedures* used (referred to as *procedural justice*) focussing on the perceived fairness of processes/procedures (including *inputs*) used to make decisions/resolve conflicts/reach outcomes – the means by which decisions are made; and
>
> *the conduct/approach* adopted (including the *manner* in which the person involved was treated) referred to as *interactional justice*) focussing on the perceived fairness of the treatment of the individual concerned, and the *information* given to the person (referred to as *informational justice*) focussing on whether the person perceived they were given adequate information at the right time.

Complying with societal expectations of conduct and decision-making will usually also mean the decision itself is a better one. If you make a decision ethically, with the public interest in mind, and in accordance with the law, it will usually be more thoughtful, more thorough, more informed, and more consistent with comparable decisions in other contexts.

Accountability

A core element of Australia's democratic system are the mechanisms by which public services are held to account to ensure that societal norms are met. These mechanisms include parliamentary oversight, court action, media scrutiny as well the involvement of bodies such as ombudsman, audit offices and anti-corruption bodies. These mechanisms can and have worked well to promote good public policy and integrity in public life. There are a number of continuing challenges which should not be overlooked.

The Parliament

Australian parliaments are effectively the ultimate determinant of what is in the public interest in any particular matter that is the subject of legislation. It would be fair to describe the current political climate in Australia as fluid with changes in government becoming more frequent and political alignment becoming more complicated with minor parties and independents have a greater role in shaping policy. It is certainly true to say that in times of instability and uncertainty the focus for those in power is maintaining it while the focus for those in opposition is acquiring it. This is not a new development. Exercising power is usually more attractive than resisting it. The desire for power has always been central to the political systems of nations with a Westminster style of government. The emphasis seems to have drifted away from those in government working to deliver the best possible services to the community, and those in opposition holding the government to account. Good policy does not seem to be esteemed by the media or rewarded by the electorate with identity politics and political spin having a much higher profile.

The political climate in Australia, particularly at the Federal level, seems to lurch from one crisis to another. Some of these crises are real and some are created for opportunistic reasons. They are fed by an apparent community desire for drama of the kind usually depicted by soap opera. Unfortunately, reality television and rant radio do not lend themselves to careful scrutiny of public policy or to effective checks and balances on the exercise of political power. These forms of media are driven by fear and the colour of conflict. The proceedings of parliamentary committees are often overshadowed by name-calling, point scoring and political posturing. If conduct of this kind becomes normalised, the task of ensuring that the public interest is being served will be subordinated to lesser partisan priorities. Committees will no longer be the 'auditors of government and guardians of the public interest' that they should be and, indeed, that the public needs them to be.[6]

The core of acting in the public interest is the need to maintain public trust. While every member of the community may not agree with a decision, and the decision may well be contrary to their personal interests, they need to have a level of confidence in the incumbent government to act in the best interests of the general community. A number of recent high profile decisions in New South Wales have not been accompanied by the level of openness and transparency that is needed to gain and maintain public trust. The result is a community that is disinterested in politics, disinclined to believe public officials and suspicious of parliamentarians of all affiliations. Given that the health of Australia's system of democracy is predicated on community participation, these are undesirable outcomes that detract from the standing of any public policy and which undermine any attempt to portray such policy as an expression of the public interest.

The Courts

The public interest is central to the role of the judiciary. In New South Wales, judicial officers swear an oath to 'do right to all manner of people ... without fear or favour, affection or ill-will'.[7] This is a reasonable, if somewhat dated, definition of acting in the public interest.

3. The public interest: ensuring good public administration and accountability | 61

The Courts are one of the only venues for close and continuing examination of what it may mean to claim that something is in the public interest. Regrettably, the courts are usually looking at what is contrary to the public interest and, in most cases, a private interest having taken precedent. Such cases often arise out of corruption investigations or shadowy matters being exposed by the media. Breaches of public trust should be publicly aired and the most serious can be addressed in criminal prosecutions. Outside of criminal cases, the challenges associated with taking a matter to court have always been time, complexity and cost. It is possible to pursue a public interest issue but the plaintiffs need to be patient, reply on good counsel and have deep pockets. Very few people will have the resources and stamina to continue with these kinds of actions to a formal determination. Tribunals have helped to make mounting such a case easier, cheaper and quicker. Tom Bathurst, the Chief Justice of New South Wales has noted, however, that

> parties cannot avoid grappling with the legislation that governs their dispute. In addition, there is an appellate process which has the potential to add a considerable layer of complexity. In fact the system of appeals from tribunals could, in some ways, be said to be more complex and confusing for litigants than the traditional avenues of appeal from a lower to a superior court.[8]

Oversight bodies

Over 30 years of working in public sector oversight I have seen extraordinary change. I have seen oversight and regulatory offices come and go. I have observed many different approaches to public sector service delivery and have tried to keep up with countless agency restructures and re-namings. I am always amazed just how many three and four letter acronym variations can be created for the same basic function.

The office of the New South Wales Ombudsman and the Audit Office have been two consistent features of the New South Wales public administration landscape during that time. More recent additions are the Independent Commission Against Corruption, the Judicial Commission, the Office of the Information and Privacy Commission and the Law Enforcement Conduct Commission. Such bodies are focussed on ensuring public services are delivered in the public interest. Their mandate is to assure the parliament that public services are efficient, effective, ethical, fair, just and most importantly, they are delivering what was intended and have not been captured by sectional or private interests.

The Media

The standard of political checks and balances and the conduct of political discourse is very closely linked to the main line of communication between politicians and the community – the media. The Internet and new information technology has prompted profound change in the management of mass media. These changes are far from ending. There will be new players and new platforms involved in the exchange of information and ideas. Ethically grounded, well-researched and accessibly presented journalism has always been an essential part of a healthy democracy. After the United Kingdom Government established an inquiry into the British media following the *News of the World* phone hacking scandal in 2011, Lord Leveson remarked when releasing his final report that

> I know how vital the press is – all of it – as guardian of the interests of the public, as a critical witness to events, as the standard bearer for those who have no-one else to speak up for them … The press, operating freely and in the public interest, is one of the true safeguards of our democracy. As a result, it holds a privileged and powerful place in our society.[9]

This sort of journalism takes time to nurture and consumes considerable resources. There is also the perennial gamble as to whether people – the consumers of mass media – will be interested and value what delivers. The alternative is the safer, cheaper and easier option. Media outlets might succumb to the temptation of reporting on topics that might be of interest to the public but which are not in 'the public interest'. In effect, the media focuses more on the private lives of celebrities than on the public lives of politicians. The former has no bearing on the public interest and ought to be ignored; the latter is critical to the public interest and warrants intense media attention.

The Public

The final stage at which we can ensure that those providing services to the community are acting in the public interest is by the community keeping an eye on them and by citizens getting involved. The extraordinary technological advances that have been made over the last decade have meant that citizens can be more engaged with government and closer connected with each other than ever before. The challenge is bringing people together at a time and in a manner when and where they actually consider the evidence ahead of a calm and rational discussion in which the various options and approaches are considered.

The Oxford Dictionary's word of the year for 2017 was 'post-truth'. It just pipped 'alt-right' as the most commonly used new word. The dictionary's compilers provided the following definition: 'relating to or denoting circumstances in which objective facts are less influential in shaping public opinion than appeals to emotion and personal belief'. We appear to live in a time when people are willing to embrace and accept opinions and conclusions that best suit them. While I am not arguing for factual absolutism and acknowledge that perspective plays an important part in observing reality, we are increasingly seeing reinterpretations of once accepted facts and complete disregard for the notion of truth. The rise of unthinking postmodernism has produced a form of uncritical relativism that is fatal to the practice of public administration. It often sounds like this: 'if you feel something is right, then it is right for you'. Facebook, Google and other massive corporations have very successfully tailored our online existence to ensure we get what we want and not necessarily what we need. Put simply, we are getting chocolate, when what we need, at least some of the time, may well be broccoli.

Eli Pariser, an online activist, detailed this concerning phenomenon in 2011. He referred to it as the 'filter bubble'. More recently, he noted that this issue has only got worse as it presents a set of serious problems:

> things that are deliberately false for political ends, things that are very slanted and misleading but not false; memes that are neither false nor true *per se*, but create a negative or incorrect impression. A lot of content has no factual content you could check. It's opinion presented as fact.[10]

Acting in the public interest will always require public discussion about what matters and why. The words that are used to explain objectives and priorities also matter. Language is a public possession and what the public understands by certain words and phrases is not mere semantics especially when the public interest needs to be set out in words. The challenge now and always will be how to achieve consensus about what words means and why some outcomes are more desirable than others in a way that allows public officials to draft and deliver good public policy. If this does not happen, public policy decisions will be made without reference to the public's aspirations. We will witness public officials behaving in a manner echoing the apocryphal tale of the French revolutionary, who saw a crowd running past, and said: 'There go my people. I must find out where they are going so I can lead them.'

The provision of alternate paths for participation may come from the innovative work being done by people like Geoff Gallop and his fellow research partners at the 'newDemocracy Foundation'. The focus is on the changes needed to deliver effective long-term decision-making that earns public trust. One option proposed at a newDemocracy event was the trial of a standing citizen's chamber, providing a voice and, hopefully a 'circuit breaker' to the current adversarial system which is often little more than an 'echo chamber'.[11]

Extending public accountability

The clear demarcation between the public sector and the private sector that has existed since Federation in 1901 has largely ceased to exist. In terms of the public interest, the big changes have involved the corporatisation, privatisation and contracting out of functions traditionally seen as public services that should not be subjected to purely commercial delivery considerations or which affect everyday life and cannot be withdrawn or withheld. These services include electrical power, water supply, delivery of disability services, provision of social housing, the operation of buses and ferries, the certification of building works, and the list goes on. In New South Wales we have also seen the privatisation of the land titles office, a proposal to privatise part of the Sydney train network, and the conferring of statutory enforcement powers on a state owned corporation. These decisions involve major changes to the conduct of public affairs and have not been accompanied by a sufficiently expansive conversation about their wider consequences in terms of the public interest.

Increasing privatisation and contracting out of services makes the role of bodies such as the Parliamentary Ombudsman more challenging and frustrating. I do not think we should be debating whether it is right and proper for the private sector to provide services that have traditionally been provided by government. We are past that point. I do not think we can or will be going back because decisions have been made that cannot and will not reversed. We are well within the stage in government evolution that Geoff Gallop has described as the 'Enabling State.' Given these substantial changes to the administrative landscape show no signs of slowing let alone ending, we must explore whether, and if so in what ways, the concept of the 'public interest' is applicable to institutions and individuals performing what were traditionally functions of government. This exploration must also include the means by which responsibility for the public interest can be carried or borne by state owned corporations and non-government entities.

The institutions I have in mind include: government owned corporations that have enforcement powers under legislation (such as WaterNSW); private sector organisations authorised to enforce legislation (such as the managers of certain gaols and detention centres, the RSPCA); government owned corporations with a business focus providing essential services such as water and power; privatised government functions (a growth area that includes management of gaols and detention centres, operation of certain bus and ferry routes, the New South Wales Land Titles Office, private certifiers performing functions under the New South Wales planning legislation); community housing providers (whose initial housing stock and tenants were originally public housing stock and public housing tenants that were transferred to them by government); non-government organisations (NGOs) funded or licensed by government to provide welfare or health related services (for example private hospitals, such as St Vincent's Hospital, and community service providers); professional organisations that are part of a statutory disciplinary scheme (such as the Law Society, Bar Council and various health practitioner regulatory bodies); private sector lawyers engaged to represent public sector entities; other persons or entities engaged by public sector entities to provide advice or other services under a contract for services; public universities; and, separate legal entities/subsidiaries established and owned by public sector entities (such as universities). While many seem comfortable taking public services into the private sector, there is some reticence by certain governments about taking public accountability measures along for the ride.

We have seen some positive developments in this regard. For example, those New South Wales government owned corporations and their staff that provide essential services are accountable through the oversight of the Ombudsman. The Ombudsman can look at whether conduct was unreasonable, unjust, oppressive, improperly discriminatory, based on improper motives, irrelevant grounds, irrelevant considerations, a mistake of law or fact. There is also accountability through the ICAC (whose jurisdiction is broader than mere illegality) and through the

Auditor-General. In other areas, calls from the Ombudsman's office for public accountability to 'follow the money' have run into a brick wall. Nowhere is this more pertinent than with the transfer of responsibility for the management of certain public housing tenants from the state housing department, FACS Housing, to Community Housing Providers. Approximately 32 per cent of the public housing stock in New South Wales is in the process of being transferred to such providers, generally including the existing tenants. Community Housing Providers had been responsible for 19 per cent of social housing in New South Wales. This is a very big change. It involves the transfer of public property worth hundreds of millions of dollars. The primary obligation imposed on those organisations is to comply with the terms and conditions of their registration as a provider and any contractual obligations they may enter into with FACS Housing in relation to the transfer to them of public housing.

We have raised with the state government our concern that the operations of such organisations are not subject to oversight by our office, whereas comparable organisations, such as community service providers, are subject to such oversight. While public housing tenants have the right to complain to the Ombudsman if they cannot resolve a problem with the housing department, once the management of their tenancy is transferred to a community housing provider they lose that right. There is no alternative equivalent organisation to which they can turn. This is not consistent. It is not fair. In my judgement, it is not in the public interest. We have raised this issue on numerous occasions, both with government and with parliamentary committees reviewing public housing in New South Wales. We are yet to see a change. This is an example of a significant public interest issue that needs close and careful attention.

My point is not that outsourcing public services is contrary to, or inconsistent with, the public interest. My point is that government and the community should approach each area with care, first acknowledging the complexities and the potential for change to be followed by complication. Outsourcing and privatisation should not be the default position. Is there any good reason why the public accountability measures developed over the years by Parliament should not be adapted to suit the new environment and provide the same level of protection the community certainly expects and deserves? The same question also applies to existing bodies with long-standing responsibility for scrutinising an area of service delivery. They must continue to apply scrutiny regardless of who is providing the service. When outsourcing a function previously performed by government is being considered, there are two questions that need to be addressed. First, how best can public interest considerations be built into the legislation and the contracts within which those functions are to be outsourced and licenced. Second, is there any good reason why existing public accountability mechanisms should not 'follow the money' as far as they remain applicable?[12]

Conclusion

The five forms of public accountability I have identified will never operate perfectly. In some instances there will be omissions and relevant factors might be overlooked. Each form has flaws and frailties because they rely on fallible human beings and the exercise of judgement that is never wholly free of personal prejudice or preference. But if each form is brought to bear on a policy consideration or a procedural arrangement, the Australian states and territories will have an effective system of public accountability that ensures that decisions are made and actions are taken by government that reflect a strong sense of the public interest.

Endnotes

1. WA Inc. Royal Commission, Volume 1, Chapter 1, at 1.2.5 and Chapter 3 at 3.1.5; McHugh JA in *Attorney General (UK) v Heinemann Publishers Pty Limited* (1987) 10 NSWLR 86 (at p191) – the SpyCatcher Case; and Mason J in *Commonwealth of Australia v John Fairfax and Sons Ltd & Ors* (1981) ALJR 45 (at p49).
2. *The Public Interest - We know it's important but do we know what it means?* AIAL FORUM No.48 (2006); *The Public Interest Revisited – We know it's important but do we know what it means?* AIAL Forum No.72 (2013).
3. For example, that where there is a statutory obligation to have regard to the public interest, this '*operates at a high level of generality*', Warkworth Mining Limited v Bulga Milbrodale Progress Association Inc [2014] NSWCA 105, at 299. Another example is that the 'expression 'in the public interest', when used in a statute, classically imports a discretionary value judgement to be made by reference to undefined factual matters, confined only 'in so far as the subject matter and the scope and purpose of the statutory enactments may enable ... given reasons to be [pronounced] definitely extraneous to any objects the legislature could have had in view", [*Sullivan v Farrer* [1989] HCA 61; 168 CLR 210 at 216].
4. Thibault, J, & Walker, L (1975), *Procedural Justice*, Hillsdale, NJ: Lawrence Erlbaum.
5. See for example: Colquitt, JA, Conlon, DE, Wesson, MJ, Porter, C,. and Ng, KY (2001), 'Justice at the millennium: A meta-analytic review of 25 years of organizational justice research', *Journal of Applied Psychology*, 86(3), 425–445; Greenberg, J. (1990). 'Organizational Justice: Yesterday, Today, and Tomorrow', *Journal of Management*, 16(2), 399; Tyler, T.R. (1990), *Why people obey the law: Procedural justice, legitimacy and compliance*, Newhaven, C.T.: Yale University Press.
6. Evans, H. (1993) 'Parliamentary Committees and the Public Interest.' *Legislative Studies*, 8 (1):15–19.
7. Oaths Act 1900 No 20 (NSW) Fourth Schedule.
8. http://www.supremecourt.justice.nsw.gov.au/Documents/Publications/Speeches/Pre-2015%20Speeches/Bathurst/bathurst_20141108.pdf
9. http://webarchive.nationalarchives.gov.uk/20140122161047/http://www.levesoninquiry.org.uk/wp-content/uploads/2012/11/Remarks-by-Lord-Justice-Leveson-29-November-2012.pdf
10. https://www.theguardian.com/media/2017/jan/08/eli-pariser-activist-whose-filter-bubble-warnings-presaged-trump-and-brexit
11. https://www.newdemocracy.com.au/docs/activeprojects/symposium/Symposium%20on%20trusted,%20long-term%20decision-making%20-%20final%20report%20(November%202017).pdf

12   This is a simple solution that has been adopted in other jurisdictions. If public funds are expended, then standard public scrutiny measures should go with it, with any necessary changes to jurisdiction or powers. This has not presented any problems in the provision of community services.

CHAPTER 4

The public interest: the essence of public leadership

Tom Frame

Public leadership is integral to shared prosperity and individual flourishing. Such leadership is able to harmonise or synchronise collective concerns and personal aspirations. Effective public leadership promotes concern and encourages commitment beyond oneself and the fulfilment of self-interest. The existence of private affluence alongside public squalor inevitably leads to social disintegration and civil strife. A society at war with itself wastes resources and squanders opportunity.

The principles and practice of public leadership deserve sustained attention and critical analysis given their abiding importance to the quality of life enjoyed by all people and in every society. Public leadership is, however, a complex phenomenon. The complexity begins with the term: first, whom or what or where constitutes the public? Second, what distinguishes public leadership from government oversight and is the former essentially about people, processes or products? The first question – the nature of the public – has prompted a number of recent works most reflecting fears that the 'public square', the place where people interact with government and each other, has been diminished, impoverished, colonised or even hijacked by malignant forces. The second question is being addressed in studies focusing on the changing nature of participation in the life of Western democracies. This chapter looks at some creative attempts to define public leadership, argues that public leadership ought to focus on advancing the public interest, and outlines the substantial challenges associated with defining the public interest in matters relating to policy and the contest of ideas that precedes both good policy development and sound public administration.

The call for public leadership

A familiar refrain in Australian public life is the lack of good leadership. This can be interpreted as a veiled complaint about the quality of recent national leadership or as a sad lament that the country lacks direction. Of course, it is convenient to attribute everything that is wrong with society to a few people and to either their inability or refusal to give everyone what they want, when they want it. Just as likely a cause for discontent is unwillingness to submit to leadership or a fickle reaction to the leaders themselves producing compliance when it proffers the fulfilment of self-interest and defiance when it calls for personal sacrifice. When asked for a brief description of what they seek in a leader or when invited to identify the essence of leadership, I doubt many Australians have given the subject a second thought let alone questioned their opinions. Perhaps it's like art: they know what they like and what they don't like but can't quite explain why. Consequently, potential leaders come and go in the public realm as viceroys, parliamentarians, heads of agencies and institutions, entrepreneurs, lawyers and the occasional academic, media personalities and sport stars until one arrives that the public seem to like for reasons that are not clear. Their influence might linger a little longer than most before they say or do something that aligns them with an unpopular or unfashionable faction or mindset and their standing begins to decline.

The rise of identity politics, the suspicion of institutions and the spread of postmodernist angst have made it difficult for leaders to exert leadership beyond the communities in which they themselves were nurtured and from which they acquire an enduring authority to speak and act. Attempts by leaders to refashion the nation or reshape popular culture are resisted if not resented with the usual litany of objections ranging from the leader's failure to speak on behalf of every sub-group and special interest organisation to the leader's inability to understand the struggles of people who are unlike them or want different things from life. Leadership has never been more difficult in a society that has never had less regard for those elected or appointed to leadership positions. As the nation slowly dis-integrates into tribes that are not coincident with the geographic boundaries of a state or a local government area, the notion of public leadership becomes increasingly more problematic as the things that divide have greater prominence than the things that unite.

Despite the difficulties and the problems, the need for public leadership is undiminished. The challenge begins with interpreting the context in which leadership is exercised and then settling on the right approach to leading so that the leadership provided is not so light that it makes no difference nor so heavy that it elicits opposition. The foremost task for public leaders is intervening without unnecessary interference, and regulating without excessive restriction. As an observer of diverse leadership styles and approaches that involve government and the development of policy, I believe a nuanced understanding of the public interest is indispensable to effective public leadership. Intuitively, this makes sense. The focus is not on the practice of leadership (which concerns means) but on what leadership delivers (which relates to ends). Before proceeding further I need to comment on competing and contrasting definitions of both the public and leadership.

Defining the public

Who or what or where are we speaking about when we refer to the public? This is a matter of considerable importance when addressing *public* leadership. We might begin by asking whether the word defines specific groups of people, a particular place or even perhaps the non-geographic realm of cyberspace inhabited by a constantly changing mix of people. The latter leads us to think about the private individual with a web-cam and an Internet connection remaining entirely within the confines of their home but making their life a very *public* spectacle or issuing provocative *public* statements to a global audience. The range of definitions is almost endless. For the purposes of this chapter, I will focus on the public as a specific group of people.

When I use the word public, I have in mind the Latin origin, *populous*, denoting a body of people who are associated (perhaps even united if the association is strong) by a common identity. This identity can relate to their joint possession of geography, ethnicity, belief or language. Drawing on the definition offered by the American educational philosopher John Dewey, people with a common identity recognise they have common concerns and organise themselves to devise shared responses. They are '*a* public'. There are, then, a number of distinct publics ranging from the undifferentiated 'Australian public' that incorporates everyone who inhabits the continent and the offshore islands as well as Australian citizens living abroad to the 'Kalaw Lagaw Ya' public comprising the 957 people (according to the 2016 national census) who are native speakers of this language (most of whom reside in the Western Torres Strait). In a socially diffuse, culturally pluralistic and technologically constructed nation like Australia, understandings of the public (or publics) are largely shaped by contextual considerations.

One final clarification: the public is better understood as everything outside the 'personal' (which relates to individuals) rather than beyond the 'private' (which can involve substantial numbers of individuals). I will juxtapose the public and the personal rather than the public and the private.

Defining leadership

The principles and practice of leadership began to be the subject of close and continuing study some two centuries ago when leadership was seen to be a decisive factor in determining military, industrial, economic, scientific, educational and political achievement. These were all public activities in which the public had a stake. Leadership was considered a public activity. It was usually based on a mandate provided by the public. Leaders relied on the willing cooperation of the public. The public usually shared in their success in small or large measure. In an age of greater social homogeneity and smaller government, most leaders operated entirely in their public realm whether they were employed by the state or represented a corporation. During the early nineteenth century, a series of leaders emerged who were able to challenge conventional thinking and received orthodoxy, to create a climate in which new thinking and different approaches could emerge, and to elicit the support of those willing to follow their example or encouragement. These individuals not only influenced those with whom they came into personal contact, they also exerted their will on the whole society.

Why they were influential and inspirational engaged the imaginations of novelists and the insights of historians eager to analyse their characters and to assess their conduct in the hope of emulating their deeds and replicating their successes. The Scottish philosopher, Thomas Carlyle (1795–1881), published the leading text of this period. *On Heroes, Hero-Worship, and The Heroic in History,* appeared in 1841.[1] Carlyle examined the lives of the prophet Muhammad, the playwrights Dante Alighieri and William Shakespeare, the Christian reformers Martin Luther and John Knox, the essayists Samuel Johnson and Jean-Jacques Rousseau, the poet Robert Burns, and the political-military leaders Oliver Cromwell and Napoleon Bonaparte. His aim was to discover the essence of heroic leadership. In his estimation this was the most attractive and effective kind of leadership. Since then, and notwithstanding the thousands of books that have been written about leadership, there is broad consensus that leadership is fundamentally about the exertion of influence.

This chapter keeps the focus on the public interest by defining leadership by its ends rather than by its means. Leadership produces movement among people. This movement is not spontaneous and may initially be opposed. More specifically, leadership is persuading people to do what they would not have done if left alone or unaided. This persuasion may involve pointing to new possibilities and inviting participation or offering to accompany people in doing things they would not have done alone. Leadership involves an element of management. Among the things they do, leaders also manage. But management is not leadership. Managers can fulfil their responsibilities without the exercise of leadership.

In thinking about the public interest, the kind of leadership I have in mind exhorts and encourages individuals to transcend their immediate and personal interests to achieve objectives that expand either the collective interests of the public or increase the aggregated personal interests of the individuals comprising the public. In effect, the public needs effective public interest policies and leadership to maximise individual and shared interests. I will expand on this preliminary definition after considering the contexts in which public leadership is exercised.

Who are public leaders?

The study of what has been termed 'public leadership' is relatively recent.[2] It has been defined in several ways. Most attractive to me is that offered by Paul 't Hart and John Uhr in their introduction to the collection *Public Leadership: Perspectives and Practices*. They begin:

> We want to understand leader*ship*, which is a particular set of activities and interactions that people in position and power *as well as other people* engage in. Moreover, we want to explore the nature of a specific, self-conscious interest in *public* leadership as something distinctive, not as some derivative or corporate leadership, nor narrowed down to executive political leadership [emphasis added].[3]

They suggest that public leadership has three main strands: civic, political and bureaucratic. 'Civic' leadership appears to cover community organisations that may be associated with the discharge of institutional responsibilities; political leadership concerns those elected to public office and comprise the legislative arm of government; and, bureaucratic leadership denotes those who hold a non-elected office of public trust. They have in mind the heads of cultural bodies, politicians and their staffers (whether in municipal councils or the national parliament), and career public servants in departments and agencies.

Notably, they differentiate between 'leadership challenges awaiting holders of public office *as well as others* aspiring to exercise leadership in the public sphere' [emphasis added]. These others denote a much broader category of leader and potentially a more expansive remit of leadership. They refer to such people as 'societal leaders' and note that the activities of these 'societal leaders' are just as much political actors as those who sit in parliaments and make laws. They include

> chief executives of non-government organisations, major corporations, social movements, organised interest groups, churches, trade unions – in short, key figures in 'civil society' who care about and/or have a clear stake in the course and outcomes of the political process and whose formal or de facto position provides them with a following, a broad audience, and/or some degree of public authority to speak and act on behalf of significant segments of society.[4]

The phrase 'as well as others', which has attracted my attention, is actually broader than these 'societal leaders'. There are many Australians who exercise leadership in the public sphere, shaping opinion and influencing behaviour, who do not hold any public office or private position. These leaders include television personalities, news journalists and radio broadcasters. Athletes, musicians, novelists and playwrights also claim insights into complex matters of policy overlooked or unimagined by public officials that affect the common life of the whole nation. These people recognize their capacity to rally support for or against a policy or decision being conscious of their ability to challenge and chastise those who hold public office. Irrespective of the extent of their experience and expertise in any matter exceeding the source of their popularity or profile, these public figures are role models for emerging youth and impressionable adults. They shape expectations of public policy and, in many respects, may be more influential in shifting opinion than those who exercise public leadership through the auspices of elected or appointed office. I refer to them as 'populist leaders' and without intending any disrespect. Their leadership is built on popular support and does not rely on the coerced endorsement that is associated with elected office. By this I mean that populist leaders are not chosen through a compulsory ballot whereas political leaders rely on the people being obliged to choose the best (or the least worst) among those offering themselves for public office.

While there are drawbacks and even dangers in allowing populist opinion to shape public policy, the values that determine the ebbs and flows of popular culture have a direct bearing on demands for public policy and on what *might* and what *can* be done by public officials in regulating what happens in the public square inhabited by the populace. Those who shape and sustain the public mood need to be conscious of their persuasive powers (if they are not already) and be responsible in the application of this power (which some are clearly not). The practice of this form of leadership might be uninformed or inconsistent. It may not be efficient or effective. But nothing is to be gained by ignoring or attacking those leading in this realm. Doing so will widen the already expansive gulf between the governing and the governed in Australia and lead to further alienation of the political and bureaucratic classes from the undifferentiated population.

A more productive response is one that identifies and clarifies the values and virtues that undergird a better-informed and more nuanced grasp of the issues confronting our society as a whole – both the formal body politic and the otherwise unregulated social community. Deliberating on thoughts and convictions about what matters precedes discussion of processes and procedures. This is what the political discourse currently lacks and seems indifferent to addressing. Hence, my contention that public leadership needs to focus on the public interest. The public interest is a term that is used freely and frequently by leaders to justify a range of opinions and outcomes. When used correctly, the public interest as a concept has enormous capacity to give focus and clarity to calls for collective action in response to common concerns.

Public leadership: a preliminary definition

Let me now offer a tentative definition of public leadership. It is differentiated from other forms of leadership in that its single-minded focus is (or ought to be) pursuing the public interest. Public leadership does not seek to preference or prejudice the needs or wants of any group at the expense of others nor does it advance personal or private aspirations and objectives to the detriment of the wellbeing of the entire citizenry. Public leadership is indifferent to polemical agendas and partisan goals, and transcends the practical preoccupations of administration and management. The discharge of effective public leadership depends upon knowledge of defining principles and familiarity with practical insights. In common with all forms of leadership, the practice of public leadership requires certain personal attributes and relies upon specific professional competencies. The attributes of the public leader are both innate and able to be inculcated through education and training. Public leadership draws on acquired expertise as well as accumulated experience of political conversation.

The best way of negotiating the critical distinction between what might be termed general leadership and public leadership is to ask, therefore, whether its exercise arises from, or has any bearing on, the public interest. If the point and purpose of a discussion is to further the interests (however these are understood) of the private lives of individuals or the culture of a private organisation rather than the undifferentiated Australian community, the discussion cannot be said to involve the practice of public leadership. If the conduct and continuation of a debate is mainly about enhancing or extending personal wealth or individual interests, this should not be considered public leadership.

Leaders and their publics

Who exercises such leadership? There are two very broad categories of public leader. I have imperfectly described them as official and non-official. In the first category is anyone employed by the state or its instrumentalities. [I want to draw a distinction here between public leadership and political – meaning partisan – leadership which is the mode of leadership usually, but not exclusively, exercised by parliamentarians and their staffers.] The focus of genuinely public leadership will often transcend the employing organisation in that appeals are often made to where or how an organisation serves the public interest and not its own health or longevity. There is a desire to locate an organisation within the wider social community and to be conscious of why and when it adds to peace and prosperity. I believe that the former Treasury Secretary, Dr Ken Henry, has been an exemplar of 'official' public leadership in that his leadership often embraces a whole-of-government, all of society mindset.

The second form of public leadership, what I have termed non-official, is exercised by anyone with a public profile who seeks to influence others. The form of non-official public leadership I want to examine is exemplary in its expression, reflective of communal values and evocative of a shared vision. It is leadership that motivates people to change their attitudes and actions or to seek a change in their personal circumstances or socio-economic conditions to allow them to do so. I regard the Chancellor of my university, David Gonski, as a non-official public leader because he does not speak for vested interests. While not discounting the place of officials, institutions and processes, those who shape popular culture and the publicly esteemed values embedded within it – for instance, educators, artists, journalists and bloggers – have not been accorded their place as influential public leaders.

These people are the 'as well as others' mentioned by 't Hart and Uhr. I have most in mind the practical leadership that exists between the exercise of institutional responsibilities and statutory procedures, on the one hand, and the direction to individuals or groups in the form of supervision or oversight, on the other. Whether non-official public leaders exercise good or bad leadership … for better or for worse, and noting the challenge of holding essentially private individuals to any form of public account, nothing is lost and everything is gained by inviting them to participate in three inter-related exercises. The first is promoting the concept of the public interest as the focus of public leadership; the second is improving our collective grasp of what the public interest entails; and the third is hosting discussions that encourage transcendence of self-interest and sectional loyalty.

The public interest

I readily acknowledge that my account of public leadership is rather 'pristine' because it relies on a shared sense of the public interest. In an open and pluralist democracy, individuals and institutions alike will contest any assertion or announcement of the public interest because the character and content of the concept remains undefined. My introduction to this collection quotes two documents that contend there is no agreed definition of the public interest. Further, they discount the need for a formal definition. Surprisingly, both documents outline a detailed public interest test.[5]

The same reluctance to define is apparent, for instance, in the development of privacy protections. The Australian Law Reform Commission's report on privacy legislation recommends that the

> Public interest should not be defined, but a list of public interest matters could be set out in the new Act. The list would not be exhaustive, but may provide the parties and the court with useful guidance, making the cause of action more certain and predictable in scope. This may in turn reduce litigation.[6]

In Britain, the Joint Committee on Privacy and Injunctions concluded that there should not be a statutory definition of the public interest, as 'the decision of where the public interest lies in a particular case is a matter of judgement, and is best taken by the courts in privacy cases'.[7]

Typical of legal dis-ease about defining the public interest is a brief remark by Chief Justice Robert French in *Hogan v Hinch*, a case heard in the High Court in 2010. His Honour stated that when 'used in a statute, the term [public interest] derives its content from "the subject matter and the scope and purpose" of the enactment in which it appears'.[8] But this approach does not help in the discussion of the public interest as a political concept relating to public policy. For their part, political scientists have also noted the difficulties associated with connecting the public interest to public policy. More than four decades ago the Australian political scientist Hugh Emy asked:

> Is it possible to place any faith in the common good [he uses the public interest and the common good interchangeably], even as an injunction to equal consideration, given the bewildering variety of rights, claims and interests in a modern society? Again, is the common good a wholly neutral concept or is it a shield to disguise the material self-interest of an entrenched and dominant class? ... Such questions go beyond the democratic model itself. They indicate that the model does not pay sufficient attention to the many-sided relationships between the individual and society.[9]

Emy claims that pluralists have 'tended to assume that the concept of public interest has lost its meaning because they cannot find any clear empirical referent for the commitment to it'.[10] He asks: should the government merely 'referee' struggles between groups so that, in time, 'a dynamic equilibrium or natural balance in which successive accommodations of group demands are seen as equivalent to the public interest'. He also noted the existence of interest groups and factions within government itself with Coalitions, parties, departments, agencies or professions all resisting consensus on what serves the public good.

Each group will press their claims and seek to make the most of their procedural advantages or tactical processes to achieve their ends. Emy's solution was this:

> Rather than try to find an inclusive empirical definition of 'public interest', we can try to show whether or not the political structure and associated processes of policy-making promote public considerations and criteria, or whether instead, they encourage private and parochial interests.[11]

The continuing challenge

Plainly, the difficulty with talking cogently and consistently about the public interest is that it means different things to different people in different settings. I want to suggest that currently we can only talk about the public interest in a very general sense – perhaps as an ideal – before we find that the application of the term becomes so diffuse that we are almost talking about different notions. In my judgement, we have done well in defining and describing principles and processes for advancing the public interest in respect of government services and their delivery. I believe there is pressing need for work on a broad conceptual account of the public interest in the development of policy. The difficulty is less with how we define and use the word 'public'. I think that can be managed by close attention to the context. The context will denote the public (or publics) most involved in a policy consideration or political decision. It is dealing with interests where we encounter a greater challenge. What is an interest and how is it protected or promoted?

As Brian Barry commented in his seminal 1964 essay, 'The Public Interest', it is a mistake to make 'being concerned about' something synonymous with an interest. Barry argues that

> a policy, law or institution is in someone's interests if it increases his opportunities to get what he wants – whatever that may be ...

> the main point about my proposed definition is that it is always a policy that is said to be 'in so-and-so's interest' not the actual manner in which he is impinged upon.[12]

The emphasis is on the intention. What actually results is predicted but not certain. The key idea is that someone believes a policy will help them to get what they want. Notably, Barry links interests to wants rather than needs implying that we *choose* our wants. The notion of interests makes us think about opportunities. Conversely, our needs are non-discretionary, we cannot do without them if we are to survive. How, then, can we rationalise or harmonise our interests so as to avoid a war of all against all?

In addressing this question, Barry draws on the Jean-Jacques Rousseau's *Social Contract* and his discussion of the 'general will' and the 'less general will' of the people which reflects the existence of a minority. Rousseau's faith in widespread civic virtue prompts 'the right question' to be asked: 'what measure [meaning policy] will benefit me in common with everyone else, rather than me at the expense of everyone else?'.[13] The force of this question is a quest for equity in the application of a policy. Rousseau contended that in a well-ordered state 'the aggregate of the common happiness furnishes a greater proportion of that of each individual'. Self-interest is fulfilled in seeking a common or public interest. As Barry notes, disagreements about the public interest are 'due only to conflicts of opinion – not to conflicts of interest'. When I decide to act in self-interest I am actually acting in the interests of all if I think in terms of 'net interests'. Further, the majority of voters are more likely to be right about what serves their collective individual interests than any given voter may be mistaken about what best serves his or her interests.

Barry argues that Rosseau's approach 'requires far more stringent conditions to be met before something can be said to be in the common interest of all'.[14] But given the existence of legitimate special interests, such as those of the very young and the very old, the infirm and the incapacitated, there are times when the public interest has to find a balance. Barry also notes that 'interests which are shared by few can be promoted by them whereas interests shared by many have to be furthered by the state if they are to be furthered at all'.[15] It is only the state that has the authority and the power to prevent the few from harming the many by promoting their sectional interests over the public interest. Public policy is not developed, therefore, on the basis of opinions but on the discernment of interests and how they are best served. The latter point – how interests are best served – is where research finds its natural place. Evidence relating to the efficiency and effectiveness of policy measures is considered in terms of a definite and known object – the public interest. Crucially, identification of the public interest was the foundational activity.[16]

The challenge of public leadership is two-fold. The first is creating an environment in which individuals are encouraged to overcome a narrow sense of their own self-interest in the expectation that the public of which they are members will be enriched by the collective pursuit of interests that are common to all. The second is building public confidence in the handling of evidence that identifies whatever happens to be the most efficient and effective means of fulfilling a common interest. Both of these tasks transcend the formal remit of parliamentarians and bureaucrats although they have a role. Without an appeal to individual values and virtues and in the absence of any spirit of community goodwill, the promotion of any policy in the public interest is liable to resentment and resistance. Without individuals in the community believing their destiny will be better served by working with rather than against others, the public interest will be little more than an empty political slogan. Leaders are key players and their leadership decisive.

Endnotes

1. *Thomas Carlyle, On Heroes, Hero-Worship, and The Heroic in History*, 1841. For the full text of all six lectures: https://archive.org/.../ThomasCarlyleHeroesAndHeroWorshipAll6Lectures.
2. For a map of recent research see Rick Vogel and Doris Masal, 'Public Leadership: a review of the literature and a framework for future research', *Public Management Review*, vol. 17, no. 8, 2015, pp1165-89.
3. Paul t'Hart and John Uhr, 'Understanding Public Leadership: An Introduction' in Paul t'Hart and John Uhr (eds), *Public Leadership: Perspectives and Practices*, ANU E-Press, Canberra, 2008, p. 3. For the full text see: https://press.anu.edu.au/publications/series/australia...government.../public-leadership.
4. Paul t'Hart and John Uhr, 'Understanding Public Leadership', p. 9.
5. Political scientists are the most reticent in acknowledging something called the public interest. Some have argued there is no public interest there are only the interests pursued by individuals and groups. An early article drawing attention to the problems associated with the public interest as a political concept is Clarke E Cochran, 'Political Science and "the Public Interest"', *Journal of Politics*, vol. 36, no. 2, May 1974, pp. 327–55.
6. See https://www.alrc.gov.au/inquiries/privacy.
7. UK Parliament, Joint Committee on Privacy and Injunctions, *Privacy and Injunctions, Session 2010–2012*, HMSO, London, 2012. For commentary see https://uk.practicallaw.thomsonreuters.com/9–518–6729.
8. See https://www.alrc.gov.au/publications/8-balancing...interests/meaning-public-interest.
9. Hugh V Emy, *Politics of Australian Democracy*, McMillan, Melbourne, 1974, pp. 82–83.
10. Emy, *Politics of Australian Democracy*, p. 166. See also G Schubert, *The Public Interest: A Critique of the Theory of a Political Concept*, 1960.
11. Emy, *Politics of Australian Democracy*, p. 585.
12. BM Barry, 'The Public Interest', *Proceedings of the Aristotelian Society, Supplementary Volumes*, vol. 38, 1964, pp. 1–38, p. 5 quoted.
13. Barry, 'The Public Interest', p. 11.
14. Barry, 'The Public Interest', p. 13–14.
15. Barry, 'The Public Interest', p. 16.
16. A very helpful study with practical suggestions on resolving disputes over what constitutes the public interest is Ian O'Flynn, 'Taking the broader view: the public interest, deliverative democracy and political ethics', in Thom Brooks, *New Waves in Ethics*, Palgrave, Basingstoke, 2011, pp. 259–77.

CHAPTER 5

The public interest: The exclusive preserve of government?

David Kemp

Is the public interest the exclusive preserve of government? My short answer is no. Given a certain definition of the public interest, public and private interest are intertwined in several important ways and cannot be prised apart. Further, even a narrow, and some would say selfishly motivated, private interest can be led towards public interest outcomes. Much will depend of course on how we define the public interest. I propose to argue that not only do we need to get clear what the public interest generally involves in a democratic state but that it is important to the future of democracy to give it some specific content – a content that hammers into place strong linkages between public and private interest. By way of warning, this discussion is going to proceed along possibly unexpected paths. I found that in thinking about the public interest and its link to non-government interests, it was not long before I came face-to-face with complicated matters of political philosophy such as the role of government, the nature of social capital, the content of the political culture, the bases for effective policy and support for democracy, and the role of political parties and leadership.

Following the line of reasoning advocated by the political philosopher Brian Barry[1], saying that something (commonly a policy or action) is in the 'public interest' is to say that it may affect any member of the public and will do so in a beneficial way. Something that is in the public interest is not merely a matter of preference; it will increase the chances that a person will be able to get what he or she wants. It is a term that points towards shared aspirations or common interests, and invites us to say more specifically what those interests may be. A further matter to note here because it is important to later discussion: in political discussion interests are possessed not merely by individual people. Collectives and institutions possess interests as well. The relationship of collective or institutional interests to the public interest is also worthy of closer examination.

The word 'public', the *Oxford English Dictionary* tells us, is 'in most of the senses, the opposite of private'.[2] The phrase 'private interest', which is also referred to occasionally as special interest, is commonly used when referring to policies or decisions which are only in the interests of a restricted number of people and which may be at the expense of the shared interests of the public. This is a very important distinction in a democracy such as Australia. In other regimes and in the period before democracy, it is and was a distinction often blurred. While narrow private, special or vested interests may be seen as opposed to broad, communal or public interests, when private interests are widely shared or held in common, their protection and advancement is generally seen to be in the public interest. In the Australian liberal tradition of democracy and given the diversity of its citizens, their shared interests have generally been considered to be life and the liberty to pursue diverse goals including happiness which generally involves attempting to influence others peacefully. Indeed, the denial of such interests can be seen as a denial of humanity itself.

If individual interests in life and liberty are the core of the public interest, then it is already evident that public and private interest are intertwined. Actions to advance shared private interests may be said to be in the public interest. This is obviously the case with constitution building which is an attempt to advance the public interest by constructing institutions that are designed to best protect these shared private interests of individuals. It is also, though perhaps less obviously, the case with economic policies and with policies providing a framework for social life as well. Before pursuing this thought further, however, a comment on the interests of institutions is warranted. When we talk of vested interests in politics, it is often with reference to institutions such as enterprises, churches, unions, lobby groups or the media, that this term is used. The basic interests of institutions can be thought of as somewhat parallel to that of individuals – to survive, retain autonomy of decision and to influence others in pursuing goals – although with institutions the matter is more complex, as other institutions cannot be said to have natural rights in the same way as individuals. Institutional behaviours may also, of course, be contrary on occasion to the rights of real persons.

Why bring the concepts of public and private interests into the discussion at all? Why not simply rely on demonstrating the costs and benefits of any particular policy, and indicating who will benefit from, or lose, from it, rather than bringing in the concepts of public and private interest? It seems to be the case that many, possibly most, policy debates occur without the terms public and private interest coming into the discussion. Some laws use the concept of the public interest, empowering some agency to use it as a criterion for decision-making (usually without definition), but most do not, even though analytically it can be argued that they conduce to the achievement of a public interest.

The public interest and democracy

Analytically the terms 'public' and 'private' interest draw attention to two important dimensions of policy: the interests that are fostered by the policy, and the breadth or narrowness of those whose interests are promoted. In a democracy these are very important dimensions. In fact, the perception of whether policy is in the public interest or only in the interest of a few may play a major role in the assessment by citizens not only of specific polices, but of governments, and indeed of the performance of democracy itself. Whether that perception is sound or accurate is another matter, underlining the conclusion that there is always a debate to be had in practice about the beneficiaries of particular laws, and how private interests and public interests intersect. For some, the fact that a law benefits corporations or unions is enough to condemn it. But there may be an argument that what is in the private interest of such entities may also be in the public interest. Not all self-interested demands are necessarily against the public interest.

The principal idea that gives legitimacy to democracy is that it is a system of government that will secure policies that have the consent of the people. Democratic constitutions embody, for example, the traditional liberal principle that taxation cannot be levied by government without a law being passed by the representatives of those who will be taxed. Such a constitutional principle is first and foremost designed to protect shared private interests in not having one's property arbitrarily removed while enabling government to advance other shared interests. It is on such bases, above all others, that government policies are accepted and from which government derives the authority to function. It is true that the people may consent to policies that arguably are in the private interest of a few. Legislators often address the particular needs of minorities and are commended for doing so. In a democracy, however, there is an expectation that the policies of elected governments will overwhelmingly be in the interests of the people as a whole. When minorities are protected it reflects the general principle that we may all be in the minority on occasion. It is an illustration of John Rawls' point that we should act as we would if we were behind a veil of ignorance as to our actual situation in the world.[3]

Claims that a government is acting in the public interest when it privileges some particular private interest have led historically to intense political debate because the truth of these claims is contested.

It is argued that some industries need protection because tariffs are good for employment opportunities; it is asserted that union rights of entry to workplaces are good because employer exploitation is prevented. These are arguable propositions. In such cases, the special interests served by the policies are clear. Contrastingly, the claim of public interest depends on more complex arguments and the impact on multiple values.

The protection of minorities is not the same as favouring minorities. Indeed, there are those who would argue that the role of government should be limited entirely to protecting shared or public interests, and that conferring private benefits on the few (usually the powerful few, especially when they are described as 'vested interests') is not what democratic government should be about. It is just such a consideration that led Adam Smith (1723–1790), the founder of modern economics, to argue that the three roles of government were protecting the country from invasion, protecting citizens from oppression by other citizens and doing things in the public good that private citizens will not do for lack of incentive. These are all things widely agreed to be in the public interest.

We can take this thought further. The most recent *Australian Election Study* shows a correlation between trends in the belief that politicians look after their own interests or those of powerful vested interests and a loss of faith in democracy. Declining trust in the performance of our democratic system may be closely linked to the belief that policy is dominated by, and is pursued in the interests of, the few at the expense of the many.[4] If this is the case, the fact not only supports the comments I have just made about assumptions as to the public interest and the role of government, but also tells us that those who ultimately will determine whether policy is promoting the public interest are the people themselves, and not governments. So there is one kind of answer to the opening question: it is not the exclusive preserve of government to judge the public interest. Ultimately it is the preserve of the people who have tasked the government and their politicians with providing a framework of laws and regulation that will achieve policies in the public interest.

This arrangement accords with the standard empirical analysis of the nature of authority relationships. As Chester Barnard pointed out in his 1930s classic, *The Functions of the Executive*, ultimately authority is subject to those who are subordinate to it.[5] It is because democratic government is reliant on authority to act effectively that this is so. Government may argue that its policies are in the public interest but it is the people who will decide. In deciding, they will consult their interests and make a judgment. But as I suggested earlier, however we define the role of government, it is not the exclusive task of government to do the things that will achieve the public interest. The shared interests of the many or even of the whole people may be advanced by private and voluntary actions that are not only in accord with government policies and the laws of the state but are unregulated and beyond those laws.

Private action can serve the public interest

The discussion of the public interest and its relationship to private interests obliges us to consider culture and, in particular, the notion of social capital which is commonly a reference to the level of trust in a society. High levels of trust increase the capacity of people in a society to express their values and achieve their aspirations. If social capital is not only trust in government but includes trust between citizens, then a culture of mutual respect among citizens, the maintenance of shared values of family welfare, opportunities for enterprise, risk-taking, innovation, and philanthropy in the private sphere, may turn out to be not just as important as sound laws and policy implementation but become the very tests of, and expected outcomes from, the laws.

Adam Smith argued in the most popular book published during his lifetime, the *Theory of Moral Sentiments* which appeared in 1759, the human quality of sympathy (empathy) and the free interactions of people in a society under just laws would lead to the development of a moral order without the intervention of the state. He thought that the well-being of society and the well-being of the nation itself, depended not only on what government did, but on what it did not do, and what it empowered its citizens to do.[6] Indeed, Smith was very clear that what government did was often not in the national or public interest but in the interests of the rulers. He remarked in another work, the *Wealth of Nations* published in 1776: 'The violence and injustice of the rulers of mankind is an ancient evil, for which, I am afraid, the nature of human affairs can scarce admit of a remedy.'[7] Nevertheless, provided that government concentrated on performing the basic functions of public administration, the lives of its citizens would continue to improve, the wealth of the nation would continue to increase, and the security of the nation against its international foes would be strengthened.

The nature of Smith's argument is highly relevant in the present context. His foremost contention was that people, in pursuing their own economic interests under just laws, by investing their capital to create new wealth would produce prosperity and revenue that would benefit all. It was as if this state of affairs was guided by an 'invisible hand'. In the terms of the present discussion, the public interest would be realised by establishing a role for government that allowed citizens to pursue their private interests. It is a subtle and persuasive argument that underlies economic theory although its cogency still eludes many. It is not an argument that has gone unchallenged. Since Smith devised his theory there are many who have sought to refute it. Yet, there are few today who would argue, as New South Wales Labor Premier Jack Lang argued in 1931, that government should take over all enterprise and plan all economic activity. Similarly, there is little contemporary appeal in asserting that, in the private economic world, employers and employees under 'capitalism' are engaged in a continuing civil or class war. That argument was well and truly lost in Australia after the 1949 Federal election that brought the newly formed Liberal Party under Robert Menzies to power. Nevertheless, we are entitled to deduce from the existence of such a debate that perceptions of shared interest and conflicting interests are ultimately matters of political commitment, policy philosophy or economic theory. I draw from these observations the conclusion that it is impossible to give content to the concept of public and indeed private interest without an overarching policy or political philosophy embodying both values and understandings of the world. It is also apparent, at least to me, that rival philosophies are not equally useful in helping us grapple with the public interest nor are they entitled to the same respect. Some theories better embody learning from experience and from classical and contemporary social and economic theory than others. Some theories are little more than wishful thinking or special pleading.

If we accept that it takes a framework of just laws, as Smith specified, and for the self-interested actions of citizens in economic life to produce a public interest – prosperity and economic progress – we realise that Smith did not argue for the pursuit of self-interest by either politicians and governments. Political life is governed by separate principles. It lacks the coordinating mechanism of the market which is essential for drawing the public interest out of the pursuit of private interests. All governments, as Smith understood them, are under huge pressures from the vested interests of the day to produce policies that will advance their narrow private interests. These policies may or may not be in the public interest. While liberal democratic constitutions are written with the goal of protecting citizens against arbitrary power, such as independent courts and checks and balances achieved through the separation of executive, legislative and judicial powers, within the institutions of government and political parties, it need hardly be pointed out that there are many opportunities for selfish and vested interests to seek to exercise influence.

To promote policies that are designed to protect or promote the public interest by drawing on the lessons of experience and the guidance of theories tested over long periods of time is perhaps the major challenge facing politicians. The danger for democracy is that citizens may come to perceive that policies claiming a public interest mandate merely reflect the private interests of politicians and their more influential constituents rather than the shared interests of the many.

The selfish interests of public institutions

There has always been the challenge for political leaders, democratic or not, to act in the public interest to secure some form of legitimacy. No political system can possibly survive without it. Legitimacy is the more or less automatic acceptance of a government's policies, what might be called its exercises of authority, by the people. In the absence of legitimate authority, persuasion is often a necessary although time-consuming substitute. When coercion or force applied on a broad scale is needed to obtain compliance, the end may be nigh for such a government. When modern dictators, such as Hugo Chavez in Venezuela or the ayatollahs of Iran, have resorted to force to maintain themselves in power, the indispensable benefits of popular legitimacy for effective government are lost and regime change threatens.

It has been argued that democracy itself should be able to avoid such problems because the people are regularly consulted through political processes: parties and elections, and the significance of the vote in constraining and directing politicians is often underestimated by those who have not experienced its power. It is nonetheless important to recognise that democracies face several structural impediments in maintaining the people's conviction that the government is acting in the interest of all. While in non-democracies the interests with access to government are few and powerful, in democracies there is a profusion of interests, of varying size, eloquence and influence. Some of these interests exert little influence; others can accrue sufficient power to become dictatorial. It is not a straightforward matter to judge the consequences of policies in mass democracies and modern complex social and economic systems. Democratically elected politicians often have weak incentives to evaluate these consequences, admit policy failure, and substitute effective policies for ineffective ones. In all cases the policies and actions – both the goals and the methods – designed to achieve both public and private interests are debatable. To the extent that debate or discussion uses concepts of private and public interest, there is always a debate of substance to be had.

When we come, therefore, to look at democracy in practice in Australia, the reality is that major political parties on which representative government relies are themselves linked in varying degrees to organised special interests. In important respects, these parties have been actually established to pursue the selfish interests of their founders, and they do so through their control over money and pre-selections especially. Again, the more government extends the scope of its regulatory activities and raises the taxes to support them, the greater is the number of institutional interests that develop within the government structure itself. These institutional interests take the form of departments, tribunals and authorities where influence is exercised often with an exceptional lack of transparency. These entities have their own selfish interests in terms of gaining greater autonomy and extended influence. They are also subject to capture by external partisan interests, both from within and without government.

It is thus an obvious error to assume that because an action is undertaken by a so-called public (meaning government) agency, that it acts always and everywhere in the public interest. The private interests of government agencies, including political parties, are often more powerful motivators of action than a philosophically justified expression of public interest. Indeed, democracy expressed as an arrangement of constitutional bodies works, to the extent that it does, by aligning the selfish interests of the politicians in being re-elected with the interests of the voters in being heard. But the Constitution provides a range of opportunities for politicians to pursue interests in ways that were not contemplated in the theory that justified the constitutional arrangement of authority. Importantly, in this regard, political parties work incessantly to increase their influence over the parliament and the electorate, and remain alert to opportunities for influencing the courts as well. In Australia, the two chamber parliaments still retain some teeth and the federal system limps along. The fiefdoms, silos and feudalisation of the public service have been the subject of frequent commentary and rightly so.

The whole tradition of political liberalism points unerringly to the dangers of unaccountable and unchecked government. While there are freedom of information and whistleblower laws that facilitate exposure of malfeasance and support law enforcement initiatives in public and private institutions, the evolution of our institutions is marked by the persistent effort of parliamentarians to press against constitutional limits and to escape scrutiny and accountability.

By way of example, contemporary political turmoil in the United States reflects a vicious cycle of declining trust producing a politics that is consumed by accusation and counter-accusation over the partisan capture of government agencies, courts, inquiries and even the so-called 'deep-state' of intelligence and security agencies. It is hard to avoid the conclusion that there is now a large task restoring bipartisan public confidence in the American system of government. How far does good government and social health depend on citizens being public-spirited by which I mean they are partially motivated to act in the public interest? Can a nation achieve outcomes that seem to be in the public interest where the pursuit of selfish or partisan self-interest is dominant? Or again, as perhaps is the case in America, what can be done when a social elite with interests not necessarily shared by the whole population dominates institutions and the principal social and economic organisations? And bringing this home to our own country: how deeply are Australians committed to the idea and the ideal of the public interest? What is their allegiance to policies that advance the public interest rather than assist private interest?

These questions direct us to the importance of political culture in identifying and promoting an arguable public interest. Given Australia's character as a largely immigrant nation which attracted people to its shores overwhelmingly by the opportunities it offered to improve one's lot in life and the chance to earn sufficient money with which to purchase both family security and material and other values, it is not surprising that Australian culture has had a strongly individualist element with a focus on private rather than public values. The Australian experience demonstrates that these values can create wealth and promote widespread wellbeing.

By 1890 and after at least half a century of public life in which there was considerable economic freedom, Australians were arguably the world's wealthiest people. But did this intense preoccupation with private affluence actually damage the public sphere by indifference to the need for a public-spirited ethos? Additionally, was the requirement adequately met for a public service to assist those who ran the state to ensure it did not become the plaything of private interest? Major General Sir George Gipps, the Governor of New South Wales, had told the members of the first partly elected Legislative Council in 1843 'that he had seen things which almost made him doubt whether the people of this colony were fit for self-government ... It was said that the people were too eager after their own pursuits; if so, would they spend their time legislating for the colony?'.

Political parties and the public interest

The Australian political leader who historically best understood that the default position of democracy was government by narrow private selfishness or powerful interests, who passionately believed in public spirited government, and the need for government to limit itself as far as possible to providing a public interest framework of laws and policies which would empower the best endeavours of an educated democracy, was Robert Menzies. The Liberal Party of which he was the principal founder in 1944 was an attempt to establish a mechanism that could achieve this.

Menzies designed the new party to ensure its members were individuals and that no vested economic or other interests could capture constitutional power within it. He articulated a policy philosophy that sought to balance a limited but purposeful role for the state with greater freedom for the private sphere. Through party discipline that would preserve this philosophy he hoped to protect its parliamentarians from the pressures of selfish vested interests. Menzies stressed that politics was not a job. It was a vocation of public service. He argued that a sense of service was the essential motivation for pursuing a life in politics. His policy priority, the area in which he invested his greatest energies, was lifting the educational level of the population. By this means, he believed the nation would enjoy better leadership of social institutions and greater support for rational policies.

How then have we arrived at a situation in which, according to the Australian Election Study, perception of public spiritedness has declined to the point that 74 per cent of Australians believe that 'people in government look after themselves'. This response is up from 57 per cent in 2007; and dissatisfaction with democracy has risen from 14 per cent in 2007 to 40 per cent at the last Federal election in 2016. There is still faith in the importance of the vote and 58 per cent still believe that the candidate for whom you vote can make a big difference although even this figure is down from 68 per cent in 2007. Why is this? Perhaps it has something generally to do with the fact that 56 per cent believe government is run for a few big interests, compared with 38 per cent in 2007; 52 per cent say that politicians do not know what ordinary people think, compared to 35 per cent in 2007. In her book on the 1996 Coalition victory entitled, *The Victory*, Pamela Williams quoted a voter from a focus group: 'we have government by minorities now. The silent majority are ignored'.[8]

Who are these big interests? Trust in politicians is exceptionally low. Recent polling shows that 74 per cent think big business has too much power, and 47 per cent think unions have, and 55 per cent want stricter laws for unions. When asked specifically on trust in the Scanlan social cohesion study, trust in unions is significantly less than trust in employers.[9] Two-thirds do not want either more spending on welfare or lower taxes – the tax/spending balance seems to be broadly accepted. While most agree that political parties are necessary to make the system work (60 per cent), minor party support has risen, and the main reason seems to be distrust of the current political establishment. In a recent monograph on the rise of minor and micro parties, the Grattan Institute concluded that the principal claim uniting them all, whether personality based or ideological, was that the 'establishment' had forfeited their trust.[10] And those who make this claim against their own democratic state around the world are not necessarily minor and micro-parties. In the United States this was the principal claim of Donald Trump and to some extent of the Democratic outsider Bernie Sanders as he condemned the system as corrupt. In France, it was the claim of Emmanuel Macron as he overwhelmed the major parties and worsted the populist Marine Le Pen. In Britain, the vote on Brexit revealed the depth to which voters rejected their traditional political establishment.

My answer to the question of whether the public interest is exclusively the preserve of government is, I trust, now clear. It rests on seven observations. First, what constitutes the public interest is always an arguable proposition. It does not differ from private interest in this regard. Second, we can only define the content of public interest policies and decisions through a coherent policy philosophy. Third, a key role of democratic debate is to agree on what the public interest is in relation to particular problems. Fourth, given the definition of interest, both policies for private and public interest will turn out to have much to do with the distribution of power – more power to the few, or the empowerment of the many. Fifth, a key function of political leadership is to offer a persuasive definition of the public interest. Sixth, a key function of political parties, so far as they can, is to develop policy philosophies to achieve the public interest. Seventh, within a framework of just laws, even the selfishly motivated pursuit of private interests can produce social and economic outcomes that benefit all. The achievement of public interest outcomes is not the exclusive preserve of government. It actually requires actions by those beyond government. It is in the public interest that government in our democratic tradition be energised by the involvement of political parties who are willing and able to pursue policies that encourage and enable private actions supportive of the public interest.

Endnotes

1. Brian Barry, 'The Use and Abuse of 'The Public Interest", in Carl J Friedrich (ed.), *The Public Interest*, Nomos V, New York, Prentice-Hall, 1962, pp. 191–204; Brian Barry, *Political Argument*, London, Routledge & Kegan Paul, 1965, pp. 190–206.
2. *Oxford English Dictionary*, XII, pp. 778–79.
3. John Rawls, *A Theory of Justice*, New York, Belknap, 1971.
4. Sarah Cameron and Ian McAllister, *Trends in Australian Political Opinion: Results from the Australian Election Study 1987–2016*, Canberra, ANU School of Politics and International Relations, p. 39.
5. Chester I Barnard, *Functions of the Executive*, Cambridge Mass, Harvard, 1937. There is a large literature on the characteristics of the authority relationship. See DA Kemp, 'Authority and Public Policy: Solving the Political problem', in H Redner (ed.), *An Heretical Heir of the Enlightenment: Politics, Policy & Science in the work of Charles E Lindblom*, Boulder, Westview press, 1993, pp. 155–186.
6. Adam Smith, *The Theory of Moral Sentiments*, [originally published 1759], Oxford, Clarendon Press, 1976.
7. Adam Smith, *An Inquiry into the Causes of the Wealth of Nations*, Book IV, chapter III, part II.
8. Pamela Williams, *The Victory: the inside story of the takeover of Australia*, Sydney, Allen & Unwin, 1997, pp. 52–53.
9. Andrew Markus, *Mapping Social Cohesion: The Scanlon Foundation Surveys 2017*, Clayton, Monash University, 2017.
10. Danielle Wood and John Daley, *A Crisis of Trust: The Rise of Protest Politics in Australia*, Melbourne, Grattan Institute, 2018, chapter 6.

CHAPTER 6

The public interest and political parties

Rodney Cavalier

The past is a foreign country. They do things differently there.

Harold Wyndham was a lifelong educationist. He became New South Wales Director-General of Education in 1952. His minister was Bob Heffron who had been a minister since 1944 and a state parliamentarian since 1930. Heffron was a former gold miner, union official, union agitator. Every teacher employed in New South Wales public schools answered to Heffron; so did the staff of the Department of Education and the specialist staffs of the State Library, the Art Gallery of New South Wales and other arts institutions. Heffron answered to cabinet, the Australian Labor Party (ALP) caucus, the ALP Annual Conference, preselectors in his seats of Botany and Maroubra, and the people of New South Wales who elected him to public office.

Neither the minister nor his permanent head had to answer to an ombudsman, an anti-discrimination board, a race discrimination commissioner or a commission against corruption. They had no cause to be inhibited about penning their thoughts to documents on files or hiring anyone other than those persons that the minister and the permanent head, in their wisdom, thought were most suitable for the job. Freedom of information was not even a thought. Quotas for women, disability, Aboriginality or anything else were beyond imagining. An exception was the office of the Auditor-General, ever present, ever real, potent and present at a moment's whiff.

Half a century ago, public interest was at the forefront of the practice of politics by those who were its practitioners. A sense of the public interest was a preoccupation for those in public office and enjoyed a far greater devotion than today as contemporary practitioners bear such a weight of oversight, second-guessing and gauntlets of approval – official and otherwise. Perhaps curiously, a sense of the public interest was stronger when elected and appointed public officials were unclouded by statutory oversight and needing to deal with institutions whose role is to protect what those institutions regard as the public interest.

Until the 1980s, and I make this observation as someone elected to parliament in 1978 and carried the burden of ministerial office from 1984 to 1988, party politics distilled and defended the public interest. Honest people from both sides of the political spectrum who sought public office were guided by the very demanding strictures of party platforms, the policies of their parties in government and a sense of what is right and wrong that was drawn from the hazards of living a life and dealing with human nature. I do not believe I am indulging in romantic after-glow about a long-lost halcyon past. Bad people abounded, cronyism replaced merit. New South Wales during the Lang era (1925–1932) was as bad as politics could be. Across the states you can all nominate bad times, such as the bulk of the years of Bjelke-Petersen (1968–1987) in Queensland. Politics sorted out the villains. Elections were cleansers.

Since the late eighteenth century, the Westminster system of parliamentary democracy has evolved to become, first and foremost, a servant of the public interest. The very structure of the Westminster system leaned towards the protection and promotion of the public interest. The executive government is chosen by the viceroy from the ranks of parliamentarians to reflect what constitutes a majority in the lower house. Each parliamentarian represents his or her electorate, pre-selectorate and party. The Northcote-Trevelyan reforms to the British civil service dating from 1854 came too late to have an impact on emerging colonial self-government in Australia between 1856 and 1859. Judges served in legislative councils, many of the key public officers were *ex officio* members of the Legislative Council. That was soon changed with greater clarity in the separation of powers and the alignment of functions. Australia had the most democratic franchise in the Westminster world by the 1860s. Adoption of Northcote-Trevelyan customs and conventions occurred across the board with no internal resistance. By 1901, the creation of a merit-based public service for the new Commonwealth was a bipartisan objective that was achieved with very considerable success.

The Westminster system shaped the first decades of federal administration in the new Commonwealth. Prime ministers used cabinets to make decisions. Effective cabinet ministers were bellwethers of the public mood and community attitudes. As a collective, cabinets were the source of ultimate authority in public administration. 'Public interest' was not a by-word. In fact, it is a term researchers would struggle to find in the examination of the records. Public interest was the unstated conception of the essential purpose of government. Why else be in government unless it was an instrument for those who held the reins of government to shape and reshape society in accordance with the beliefs and values of the governing party? Our democracy became stronger because government existed to serve the public interest and was understood to serve the public interest. If the ruling party failed to do so, the people elected a party fielding candidates that did.

Australia's democracy is founded on institutions that have enabled the nation to surmount the collective failure of its political parties. These institutions have provided sound public administration when the political process has either lost its way or become self-obsessed.

I have in mind the Treasury, the Reserve Bank of Australia, the Australian Taxation Office, the Australian Bureau of Statistics, the Australian Electoral Commission, collecting institutions (such as the National Library, the National Archives and the Australian War Memorial that preserve the documentary record of our nation, however inconvenient the documents might be), an independent judiciary composed of personnel qualified to serve and the armed forces subject to civilian control. Some governments have shown tragic disrespect for these critical underpinnings of Australian democracy in the form of reduced appropriations which both the ATO and the ABS have endured with direct consequences for the integrity of their functioning. A number of incoming Federal governments have terminated the appointments of departmental secretaries and replaced them with individuals considered more sympathetic to the government's plans and priorities. This happened when the Whitlam Labor Government was elected in 1972 and the Howard Coalition Government came to office in 1996. These are very significant actions with the potential to alter the place of the Australian Public Service in national affairs. Australia has not reached the same stage as the United States in which a head of government places operatives at the head of departments with the express purpose of destroying them. That possibility is far from fantasy.

If reminders are needed, and I suspect they might, Australians must understand that democracy is, by definition, a servant of the public interest. The people decide who governs and they expect their collective and individual interests to be advanced. Commentators might dislike the policies political parties take to the electorate and abhor the promises they make to voters. They might not like the government the people elect and their reasons for doing so. But the public get to decide who will represent them and act on their behalf. No one gets to second-guess the will of the people. Australia's electoral laws are designed to enrol the citizenry and oblige their participation in the democratic process. No contemporary Australian polity engages in voter suppression and electoral fraud is considered a serious indictable offence. Yet, manipulating the electoral system is a common feature in many parts of the United States, one of many signs that America is a failing state.

While Australians might be critical of American politics and its conduct of democracy, the Westminster system is also under threat. The foundations of Western democracy are being destabilised as more and more people agitate for change outside the realm of traditional, formalised political processes. Populism is one explanation for its decline. In Australia where the two major parties command three-quarters of the electorate's vote and all citizens aged over 18 years are compelled to vote, the situation has not yet descended to the travesty it has become in the United States. Amid much that is wrong, the Westminster system – with its overlay the Australian system of adversary parties – is likely to prevent a tyrant emerging.

Australian party politics have actually gone in the opposite direction to populism. Parties are closing in on themselves, restricting membership, seeking wherever they can and however they can, to exclude ordinary party members from a meaningful role in decision-making. Taxpayer funding of parties has enabled machine managers to eliminate any substantive role for members. They are increasingly unnecessary and, one wonders, whether some party officials would prefer they did not exist. Parliamentary parties have become spaceships that touch Earth from time to time but not for renewal and not for intellectual sustenance. Connection with the party membership is pure ritual; applause is expected and assumed. Commanders will decide the composition of their crews. They will determine who comes on board and who is required to disembark. Parties are on the verge of becoming self-sustaining oligarchies. The ranks of parliamentarians from one side of politics are currently drawn exclusively from a political class. People from the world of work are disappearing from our parliaments as they are from the leadership of trade unions.

By the 'political class' I mean those operatives who depend on the party organisation for their income, sense of self-worth and social standing. In the ranks of Labor, but increasingly among the Liberals and Nationals as well, the political class is the principal source of parliamentary representation. The people I have in mind include: the staffs of ministers and parliamentarians; salaried party officials; trade union leaders and those working for business and industry groups; and, the employees of so-called 'think tanks' that exclusively serve the interests of one side of politics. There are also the principals and staff of specialist lobbyists, public relations firms and election campaign specialists (these three categories often merge into one) who are dependent upon their side being in government to pay wages and fund programs. The gene pool is restricted and self-replicating. In the natural environment, a concentration of so many like genes heralds species death. In sum, an aspiring candidate has to be on the inside to have any real show of winning pre-selection for a safe seat. Celebrity candidates or those preferred by head office are imposed on an electorate, local selection processes are over-ridden to avoid the wrong result.

At a dinner hosted by the Werriwa Federal Electorate Council of the Labor Party, Gough Whitlam observed on the fiftieth anniversary of his election to the House of Representatives that he could not win pre-selection in the modern Labor Party: 'I was neither a union official nor a parliamentary staffer nor a relative of a Labor parliamentarian.' I have no doubt that a barrister or any other professional in a demanding practice could not win Labor selection for a safe seat anywhere in the country. Gough was one of eight candidates who nominated for Labor selection in the seat of Werriwa in 1952. Each of the eight candidates had real jobs in the community. We tend to recall Gough as an eminent barrister before entering parliament. He was also a husband, father of three, and held leadership positions in the Cronulla South Parents & Citizens Association, the Cronulla Returned Service League (RSL) sub-branch, he was a delegate to the district council of the RSL and was a member of committees for Port Hacking Rowing Club, Cronulla Torch-Bearers for Legacy, Cronulla Boys' and Girls' Library and Craft Association, Sutherland Shire Auxiliary of Sydney District Nursing.

People from the world of work – both professions and trades – once dominated parliaments. Such a person need not apply now. In the current (2018) Senate, the entire Labor contingent are either former union officials or liegemen of a union bloc. There are no mavericks whether blue or white collar in their pre-parliamentary life. Almost without exception, the union officials-cum-parliamentarians have never worked in a real job. By 'real' I mean a job in which it is a sackable offence to advance the interests of the Labor Party during normal working hours. Where does a notion like the public interest figure in the arc of career ambition for the coming operative? I suggest very little, if at all. Advancement depends on mouthing the orthodoxies of a culture of obeisance and shifting the sounds (with whatever finesse can be mustered) as the prevailing orthodoxies change. Operatives move through the ranks until they crack the inner-circle of leadership after which they perpetrate the orthodoxies and ensure their enforcement. The prospect of original thinking in such a cloister is minimal. Creativity and initiative are unwelcome and discouraged.

We must look at what is happening to the historic catchments of the parties of labour and capital. The royal commission into the banks and the financial services sector is revealing that boards have withdrawn from questioning themselves and management. Oversight is minimal. Profit growth appears to be the principal preoccupation. The revelations of malpractice and greed are little different from the total breakdown of internal scrutiny and audit within the Health Services Union. The royal commission into the building industry featured revelations that the Australian Workers Union (AWU) was building membership numbers (mainly for the purpose of claiming additional delegates at ALP conferences) through sweetheart deals with selected employers that had the effect of depressing wage growth.

What might these collective failures of governance and character have in common? I suggest an absence of experience of the work involved in banking at lower and middle levels. David Murray, a saviour in the past and again one hopes, began his career as a teller in a suburban branch of the Commonwealth Bank. Once it was a given that the leadership of the AWU had worked in shearing sheds and underground in hard rock mines. Now such people are an extreme rarity. Do you think a union official who had mopped the floors of hospitals would so blithely spend on herself the hard-earned union dues of her once fellow workers? The modern official, living inside a culture of entitlement, did not ever work with orderlies in hospitals. Workers had not ever been either their friends of colleagues. Board members proclaim that their knowledge of management is a generic skill. This proficiency is apparently superior to knowing how workers in the company deliver profits. Union leaderships are so often political operatives suffering a rite of passage to their true calling as ministers in a government.

The result of this widespread inbreeding is those elected to parliaments across Australia are overwhelmingly from the only class that has survived into this century – the political class. As a coherent grouping they fulfil all of the Marxist definitions of class: consciousness of each other, action in concert, action to advance themselves and their class against all others. An abstraction like the public interest is not a preoccupation on the way up for those coveting parliamentary office. On arrival, the public interest is one phrase among many in the stroke play that rhetoric requires.

These attributes stand in complete contrast to those that made Neville Wran a master practitioner of the politics of the possible. He was forever pushing against the frontiers of what was possible. He did not use phrases like the public interest. That was not Neville. He preferred to challenge, if not unsettle, ministers and public servants by asking: 'what's in this for Joe Blow and his missus?'. You could not answer that with a Powerpoint slide or rummage through your departmental briefing for the numbers. You needed to be across the case for and against a proposal to convince the Premier of the need for what you were seeking from Cabinet. 'Joe Blow and his missus' were representative of the vast majority of the citizens of New South Wales and those for whom the Wran Government sought to legislate.

On both sides of politics, the great leaders have always been conscious of the public interest. Their approach is to ask a question that obliges a return to the basics: who benefits from a policy or decision? In a time of great social division, the British Prime Minister Benjamin Disraeli wanted to know how a legislative measure preserved a conservative hegemony without breaking Britain into two nations. Great peacetime leaders of the political Left, such as Attlee, Chifley and Whitlam, asked whether a policy or decision redistributed opportunity so as to create a fairer society. They believed that Jerusalem was an achievable reality. A consistent thread through the Menzies years, a thread that was as strong in 1966 as it had been in 1949, was securing regional stability and global peace, sustaining a public sector that delivered services efficiently to the people, maintaining a sense of the nation and its sovereignty, enhancing respect for the rule of law and improving the outcomes of the democratic process.

Having a grand ambition was critical. The promotion of a grand ambition placed public interest at the forefront of political life. Robert Menzies speech on the 'forgotten people' during 1942 was a crystalising of his personal and political values, forged out of the bitterness of party rejection, an understanding of past error, the need for the non-Labor forces to build bridges to potentially unaligned segments of the electorate. The Whitlam Government's programs can be traced to Gough Whitlam's public addresses and published works. His ideas spanned reflection on the Commonwealth powers referendum of 1944 to the provision of housing, the distribution of population and the decentralisation of government after his election to parliament. Whitlam was attentive to the changing demands being imposed on public administration and the need for government to be agile and innovative in the development of public policy.

The policies of a not so distant past were built on values that were themselves forged in political discourse, intellectual clash, extensive research, a knowledge of history and a familiarity with the processes of democracy so that every participant could take pride in an outcome whose ownership they shared. Serving the public interest was the outcome whether it was expressed or unexpressed, implicit or explicit. Creating an Australian democratic tradition within the colonies after 1856 and in the Commonwealth after 1901 was a remarkable achievement. Practicing democracy while building a nation is wholly different to manufacturing a brand and selling products via qualitative polling and focus groups. Promises based on polling are no more and no less than offering the punters what they have professed they want but about which they could be mistaken.

Moral authority is not a quality we associate with modern leadership, especially in the political realm. Practitioners no longer seek to persuade the electorate of the need for a controversial policy or a painful decision. Politicians have lost the faculty of persuasion. They speak at the electorate when they are not playing mind games. Whatever the state of perceived opinion and the prevailing appeal of one policy over another, Arthur Calwell opposed conscription, Ben Chifley believed in nationalising the banks, HV 'Doc' Evatt fought against outlawing the Communist Party, John Gorton expanded the realm of Commonwealth activity, John Howard took an unpopular position on the sale of Telstra and introduced a Goods and Services Tax (GST) after John Hewson had lost the 1993 election proposing exactly the same thing. Effective policy advocacy required a leader to take on internal opposition, adverse polling and pre-existing majority opinion. Leadership was about changing minds if the public interest was actually best served by an unpopular measure. Such advocacy now demands our admiration because advocating the unpopular is foreign to our contemporary political culture.

Serving the public interest has never been about pandering to the lowest common denominator. Serving the public interest requires leadership, values and the capacity to persuade a majority within the electorate that your policies make sense and your vision is worthwhile. We are living in an age that is post-Belief in which political contests and election campaigns have become an auction. With belief passé, our leaders stumble in a values-free void. Polling is seized like a lifeline.

Since 2007 Australia has endured the most sustained period of bad government in the history of Federation. A political class has colonised the staffs of ministers, party leaders and members of parliament. As the last link in the flow of advice that ultimately reaches a minister, these people dominate modern governance. Political staff in our parliaments have more in common with staff on the other side of the aisle than they do with the branch memberships of the parties that notionally they serve. At the apex of parliamentary politics, in my view exacerbating all that is bad about modern governance, is the emergence of a Godhead as party leader who will either lead the party from the captivity of opposition to the freedom of the Treasury benches or lead a struggling government from electoral oblivion to longevity by putting its adversaries to the sword. In a Labor Party that was once ruthlessly democratic, no decision is now so important that it cannot be quietly resolved in camera. Constructive criticism of the kind that was essential to internal coherence and the development of a sound policy platform is now forbidden. No decision of importance will ever require more people than can fit around a standard-size banquet table in a Chinese restaurant. Conferences are mere theatre. The captain's call, a prerogative that renders the party room irrelevant, was unknown until recently. It is now taken for granted and party leaders can set direction by personal fiat.

These developments are inconsistent with the traditional governance of political parties and the norms of democratic conduct. Power unimaginable even in wartime is now concentrated at the top. A values-free political class inhabits the nation's parliaments and has assumed control of the flow of advice. The experience and expertise of a professional public service has been sidelined in much decision-making. Case studies of this degeneration and the damage it has caused include former Prime Minister Kevin Rudd's pronouncements on hospital 'reform' and the need for a mining tax and former Prime Minister Malcolm

Turnbull's refusal to contemplate curbing capital gains tax concessions and floating the idea that the states might be granted taxation powers. Rudd and Turnbull are remarkably similar in arriving at the top of their respective parties with heightened expectation of what they could achieve and then squandering their opportunities because they acted unilaterally and pre-emptively without sound advice. These episodes would not have been remotely possible if Australia enjoyed a system of cabinet government of the kind the founding fathers of the Commonwealth certainly expected.

The contrast between the quality of politics in the 1890s and now could not be more stark. The Federation was created by plebiscites being carried in all six colonies. The Constitution was endorsed by a majority of electors in all colonies. A nation came into existence that achieved sovereign independence and took its place in the world of nations. Little that lay ahead would be straightforward and nothing was pre-ordained. There were no detailed blueprints that assured national success. Nor were there tried and tested models of participatory democracy that simply needed replication. Two world wars, economic depressions and recessions, and plenty else that went wrong provided experiences that educated and re-educated generations of those who lived in the shadows of these cataclysmic events. Amid internal and external conflicts with the potential to divide the nation and damage its democratic foundations, parliamentarians sought to serve their party and the nation. They could serve their party *and* the nation because the public interest was as one with the cherished values of their party. Parties were, of course, seeking re-election. In my experience, electoral success was an outcome incidental to achieving good government. Winning the next election has become the political obsession of this century. Perhaps it was always this way. I'm not sure that it was. Winning had a reason beyond the mere retention of power and securing the accompanying trappings of privilege. Winning used to be a beginning. So, what needs to change?

Only intensely practical measures will end the rule of a political class. First, abolish taxpayer funding for election campaigns and party administrations except for those parties that are able to demonstrate the party membership is in control. Second, restrict union office to those members who have worked in the industry for a minimum five years full-time. Third, make it a criminal offence for ministerial staff to instruct public servants. Fourth, the decision to make donations to political parties will require the express approval of the shareholders and union members. In sum, enrich the catchments and you will enrich party selections. In time, parliaments will again possess leadership contenders worthy of the Australian nation and its people.

CHAPTER 7

The public interest and public sector priorities

John Uhr

Introduction

This chapter uses a series of brief historical case studies to illustrate what public sector officials think they *can* and *should* do when reflecting on 'the public interest'. It helps to know that Australian analysts of public sector reforms have often looked very closely at debates over the public interest.[1] It also helps to know that Australian social scientists have written some of the best international accounts of how to 'institutionalise' the public interest.[2] In this chapter my focus is, however, more practical. Two of my cases relate to elected representatives in parliamentary systems and two of my cases relate to appointed public servants – one case from the United Kingdom and one from the United States. I am not searching for a comprehensive theory of the public interest. My aim is to use selected cases to help students of policy and governance to reflect with greater purpose on the institutional settings in the public sector that provoke claims and debates over what is and what is not in the public interest.

My hunch on a 'theory' about the public interest is that the concept arises from modern liberal philosophy's fear of 'sinister interests', to use

Jeremy Bentham's term to describe socially-noxious and therefore misplaced private interests.[3] This brand of liberalism is grimly realistic: it assumes that we all have powerful self-regarding interests tempered by very weak socially-regarding inclinations. In this world of competitive self-interest, the concept of the public interest serves as a prudent precaution against undue reliance on the presumed good will of any individuals or groups holding and exercising political power. The concept of the public interest serves as a protective safeguard against deceptive misrule. The concept is a procedural protection against exercises of ruling power which have yet to demonstrate their *bona fides*: which is not so much their legitimate authority as their genuine interest in what used to be called the common good. The concept of the public interest is not, as often alleged, reactionary: think of it more as a *reactive* right against what we might fear of as *proactive* might.

Case One: Australian Chief Ministers

My first case study draws on a brief account of Sir Henry Parkes. He was 'the father of Federation' we are reliably told by contemporary chroniclers. Parkes was the premier of New South Wales for many years before Federation: half a dozen years in the 1870s, another four years in the 1880s, and through to his final year as premier in 1891. In the year after this eventual retirement, and a few years before his death in 1896, Parkes composed his foremost literary work, *Fifty Years in the Making of Australian History*.[4]

Parkes was a seasoned political fighter who knew from hard experience how to manage political parties – how to lead them and how to weaken political oppositions. Yet in this very long work, Parkes records among his closet friends many literary figures, notably Charles Harpur: like Parkes, a poet; unlike Parkes, a major poet. Parkes went on to publish several volumes of his own poetry (or verse), displaying many elements of a keen literary competency that we also encounter in *Fifty Years in the Making of Australian History*.

In the penultimate chapter, Parkes presents a 'review of my political life'. In a lengthy examination of his role in the evolving self-governing system of responsible parliamentary government, Parkes tries to draw out some of the larger lessons from what he has seen and done. One of these relates to the concept of the public interest. In what he calls 'my intercourse with the civil servants of the country', Parkes notes that he treats them 'with uniform courtesy as gentlemen' (such then where the times) 'while observing that distance which is necessary to enable the Minister to say "yes" or "no" in the public interest'.[5] The implication is that the civil service lacks the authority to make judgments that require a determination of the public interest. This implication holds that the system of responsible parliamentary government is the source of the authority to confer that determining power to responsible ministers: that is, ministers who are constituted to respond 'yes' or 'no' when provided with advice from the civil service.

The context of Parkes' account is relevant because he speaks here 'as an administrator' by which he means a public official who administers (or 'ministrates') civil services. Parkes contends that there are 'many unseen influences in the public service' which can come into conflict with a minister's interest (private interest?) in 'economy or reduction'. According to Parkes, these 'unseen influences' 'therefore had to be guarded against'.[6] The relevant principle was that the power of government had to be shared between political officials and civil officials: with civil servants *advising* and ministers *deciding*.

Well, not exactly. Parkes takes as an example the New South Wales public works framework where a ministerial proposal for new public works would be 'prepared by his officers'. In most normal circumstances, the proposal would be endorsed by 'the political majority supporting the Government' often, Parkes says, 'with little or no inquiry'. Parkes' reflections on the concept of the public interest caused him to reform this process so that ministers retain responsibility for whatever policy or program they are introducing. In the reformed process, the proposal would then go to a committee 'drawn from both Houses and both sides', with this parliamentary committee having the power to determine the fate of the minister's proposal. Parkes claimed that 'the principle of Ministerial responsibility' can work together with 'the principle of Parliamentary authority over Government'. This claim is made with one important qualification that is Parkes' warning that 'so long as the integrity of the law is maintained'.[7]

Here we see the vital relationship between *forms* of public interest and *substances* of public integrity. Two very real threats to this sense of public integrity should be noted. First, a weakness in ministers to loosen their official responsibility by allowing other members of parliament (such as concerned local members favouring, for example, a railway line) a right to refer proposals to such a parliamentary committee. Second, misguided ministers with 'some notion of securing professional competency' substitute 'a committee of experts' (perhaps a 'deliberative jury' in contemporary language) for the parliamentary committee. Such action would, according to Parkes, defeat 'the one transcendent principle of the authority of Parliament in the expenditure of the national revenues'.[8]

One of Parkes' conclusions was that the emerging Australian system of parliamentary government was only as strong as its weakest link. He had in mind the fact that 'the world contains weak-minded and bad men'. The process of self-government 'must be protected from impurities'. Here Parkes notes that political parties are not by definition 'impurities'. What he terms 'the nature of the interests at stake' in politics can be regulated through 'honest and open debate by opposing sides' – that is, not simply by the force of a governing party. The real source of mischief affecting parliamentary government are 'the pretenders' within each political party who plot their pathway to 'public distinction' through public deception far removed from the qualities of 'purity and integrity' required to establish and maintain a 'sound and healthy public spirit in Australia'.[9] Notably, Parkes' defence of the parliamentary determination of the public interest has many qualifying terms and conditions. The main point is not that elected representatives have greater intellectual skills than unelected bureaucrats. It is subtler than that. He thinks that elected representatives generally have wider *deliberative* responsibilities as members of a parliament. Their role is to debate the disputed nature of the public interest as elected community representatives.

Case Two: British backbenchers

The two terms 'Westminster' and 'Whitehall' refer to two power centres in the British system of government.[10] The term 'Westminster' typically takes precedence over 'Whitehall' because the civil service is considered accountable to 'the government of the day' comprising the party or parties possessing the confidence of Parliament, to whom the governing ministry is itself accountable. This system of cabinet government includes a large number of ministers, each exercising the primary demands of accountability over civil service agencies under their allocated responsibility. Seen from the perspective of the ordinary civil servant, the minister individually and the ministry collectively hold the reins of accountability, exercising formal authority over the bureaucracy and taking formal responsibility before Parliament for the performance of that bureaucracy.

To use traditional Whitehall language, civil servants are 'anonymous and invisible' for most public purposes, taking whatever official responsibilities are given to them by ministers, to whom almost all of their professional accountabilities are owed. That, at least, is a traditional theory of civil service accountability favoured by career officials. The reality is considerably less tidy with competing lines of accountability cross-hatching the bureaucracy with many pressure points. For the most part, the system carries on well despite discrepancies between the idealised expectations of ministerially-based accountability and the realised expectations of competing accountabilities.

An outstanding example of non-compliance with standard expectations relates to Winston Churchill, perhaps Britain's most esteemed political leader in modern times. During most of the 1930s, Churchill was out of favour with his own governing party (the Conservatives), holding no ministerial office and serving as a non-ministerial backbencher, with no official authority or rights over the civil service.[11] Churchill's major policy cause at that time was to bypass the wishful-thinking of 'appeasement' by restoring British re-armament in the face of the rising threat from the Nazi regime in Germany. Churchill repeatedly showed that the British government's claims about defence preparedness were inaccurate and misleading. His main fear was that the public was being deceived by inaccurate government information intended to lull them into a false sense of security.

To cut through government-induced public complacency, Churchill needed more precise information on Nazi war preparations and British unpreparedness to respond. The source was close at hand. During the 1930s increasing numbers of civil servants (including serving military officers) became covert providers of government information to Churchill. Some leaked confidential information, others handed over copies of government documents, some prepared their own written briefing papers, others briefed Churchill personally but confidentially.[12] All turned to Churchill, persuaded that their accountability to the government of the day was *conditional* rather than *categorical*. Even the cabinet secretary, Sir Maurice Hankey, initially lent his private support, covertly praising Churchill for demonstrating public leadership that the government could not muster. Others, like the Foreign Office's Ralph Wigram went much further, meeting and briefing Churchill frequently, sometimes with the acquiescence of top officials. Churchill was later to praise Wigram for 'his courage, integrity of purpose, high comprehending vision' and to honour him as 'the epitome of courage and farsightedness'.[13]

Of course, not all civil servants saw things so conveniently or consistently. The best example is the cabinet secretary. Hankey initially tolerated Churchill's remarkably unorthodox working relationships with career civil servants. To those who suspected that helping Churchill was acting contrary to the convention of civil service loyalty to their ministers in the government of the day, Churchill warned with these remarkable words: 'You must realise that loyalty to the State must come before loyalty to the Service'.[14] Senior officials like Hankey were conscious of both sides of the question but eventually began to lose support for Churchill's remarkable reliance on leaked official information. Churchill's defence was that he was using such information 'in strict confidence', providing it to those inside ministerial government 'in the public interest'.[15]

Standing back from the fascinating details of this case study, we can see that it all turns on competing interpretations of 'the public interest' and on how different officials understand loyalty to 'the State'. In the British context, and across the Westminster-derived world generally, traditional concepts of 'officers of the crown' have always had the potential to separate out accountabilities owed to 'the government' and to 'government' as such. If 'the state' is an abstract concept and one that is difficult to operationalise, then 'the Crown' can work more concretely in those constitutional monarchies (in and beyond Westminster) where an idealised accountability to the crown can limit aspects of accountability owed to the ministry, itself conceptualised traditionally as 'the crown's advisers'.[16] These opaque constitutional conventions are rarely replaced by transparent public law.

Looking back, we can see that this practice of eliciting public-interest disclosures was not Churchill's only use of the public interest concept during the 1930s. In 1933 he had published the first volume of his monumental biography of his ancestor, John Churchill, First Duke of Marlborough, which has several important references to the public interest. These references are not quotations from Marlborough but references by the author (Winston Churchill) to Marlborough's reliance on public interest concepts to navigate his own course of action during the regime change at the end of the Stuart era. The Glorious Revolution of 1688 brought in political and administrative changes of immense proportions for Marlborough who had to transfer his high public responsibilities from one head of state to another. Churchill describes

Marlborough as 'a kind of prime minister' or virtual prime minister before the formal arrival of that office under Robert Walpole from 1721–1742. Churchill uses Marlborough to illustrate many political virtues, one of which is the quality of sound prudence to know which way to turn when searching for the larger public interest.[17]

Case Three: American civil servants

After the 1968 election of Richard Nixon as the President of the United States, many career officers in the civil rights division of the Department of Justice were perplexed about their rights and responsibilities as public servants. They eventually decided 'to revolt' against what they saw as misguided and possibly unconstitutional policy by the Nixon administration to delay implementing United States Supreme Court orders for immediate school de-segregation in the southern states of the Union. The civil rights officials had earlier taken their oath of office which they now read as authorising their 'revolt'. That oath called on them to 'support and defend the Constitution' and to 'discharge the duties of the office' well and faithfully, as the language puts it. Notably, 65 of some 74 Justice lawyers signed a memorandum of protest to the newly appointed head of their division. This protest noted the federal civil-rights statutes as the ground for the Court's orders on de-segregation and feared that 'public faith' in American constitutional systems would be eroded by new government policy.[18]

The American civil servants continued their 'revolt' because of what they understood to be their oath-bound 'obligations to their profession and to the public interest'.[19] Claiming that the Attorney General had 'no discretion' to delay or even bypass the Court order, the civil servants decided that they would not resign. Instead, they would not accept or implement government policy on delayed de-segregation. Again claiming 'to represent the public interest', they refused to follow government directions or to comply with the Attorney General's odd and provocative statement that: 'Around here the Attorney General is the law'.[20] This assertion of authority did cause a number of the revolting lawyers to resign. Others remained in office and effectively engaged in a form of civil disobedience.

This case is important because it blends two types of oaths bearing on the public interest. The first oath is the constitutional oath of office required of executive officials. This oath means that career officials orient their way according to their declared duties to uphold and promote the constitution. Such an understanding of their duties could potentially bring them into conflict with whatever position their cabinet secretary or agency head might hold or promote. The second oath is the professional oath taken by lawyers. It is fundamentally an oath of loyalty to the court system as distinct from loyalty to client or employer. Thus, it is not very hard to find this and many other case examples illustrating public interest dilemmas in the American system of national governance.

Case Four: British civil servants

During the 1980s, the so-called 'Ponting Affair' prompted a return to the issues raised during the 1930s Churchill saga. Clive Ponting was a Ministry of Defence official who broke ranks and followed in his predecessors' footsteps by briefing parliamentary representatives. In this instance the briefings were about the Thatcher government's allegedly misleading public statements about the 1982 Falklands War.[21] The Thatcher government brought the full force of legal accountability against Ponting, only to watch a jury acquit him in the belief that civil servants did indeed have higher obligations to help parliament hold governments accountable. After that horse had bolted, the British civil service hierarchy reformulated its own professional code of conduct to re-state the traditional doctrine that civil servants owe their primary duty of accountability to the government of the day: a doctrine later reshaped by the Blair government when modernising this principle along with many other aspects of civil service organisation.

Ponting's dilemma was this: believing that his public service agency was not providing comprehensive information to ministers as they responded to parliamentary questions from Opposition members, he thought that deliberately withholding information (justified by reference to national security) was forcing ministers to mislead Parliament. Ponting did what he could to protest within his agency but with little success. His contention was that public servants were helping ministers 'evade their responsibilities to Parliament'. Ponting resolved his dilemma by releasing information to members of Parliament without authorisation. This action triggered the prosecution against him for breaching the *Official Secrets Act*. When surprisingly acquitted through a sympathetic jury, Ponting stated what he considered was the larger principle at stake: civil servants 'must ultimately place their loyalty to parliament and the public interest above their obligations to the interests of the government of the day'.[22]

The Head of the Home Civil Service, Sir Robert Armstrong, produced 'A Note of Guidance on the Duties and Responsibilities of Civil Servants in Relation to Ministers' in 1985 in response to the court case. The 'Armstrong Memorandum', as it is widely known, set out the revised post-Ponting constitutional doctrine relating to civil service responsibility. That formulation was itself revised in the late-1990s to take account of the Blair government's civil service code of conduct. But the core principles remain as formulated by Armstrong, with no explicit acknowledgment of any higher loyalties to the public interest, however that might be discerned. The civil service 'has no constitutional personality or responsibility separate from the duly constituted Government of the day'. The civil service is 'a non-political and professional career service'; civil servants must serve ministers 'with integrity and to the best of their ability', in the hope we note that they will act so as to maintain 'the confidence of Ministers'. In 'the determination of policy', civil servants have 'no constitutional responsibility or role distinct from that of the Minister'. Civil servants will 'damage their integrity as servants of the Crown' if they lose that ministerial confidence or otherwise cause doubts that they might be 'forfeiting the trust' placed in them.[23] We also note that contrary to Ponting's misguided sense of his high public office and public trust, the Armstrong doctrine holds that the relevant trust is ministerial, not public or parliamentary.

Puzzles of public leadership

In my brief discussion of the leadership dimensions of the public interest, I am guided by my former Australian National University mentor, Professor Peter Self. Many of Self's highly regarded books on policy and public administration contain references to the public interest. For instance, Self's *Administrative Theories and Politics* refers with some distaste to the public interest pretensions of 'centralising European monarchs' and a preference for pluralist alternatives. Yet, Self refers a page later to the obligation on civil servants 'on rare occasions to resist a ministerial command' and provides interesting examples of individuals breaching 'administrative propriety'.[24] Self also provides a guide to public interest theories with a rejection of 'a narrow pluralist view' confined to procedural rules. This element of his work reflects a move from theories of *distributive* to *substantive* justice, with a critique of 'utilitarian theories' that value 'the aggregation of sectional interests' ahead of alternative theories that avoid such a 'summation of the parts'. Again through examples, Self defends a model of the public servant as 'a moderate protagonist for certain interests which have perhaps implicitly been entrusted to him for reinforcement', such as national economic solvency or the efficacy of environmental protection.[25]

An early illustration of Self's approach to the public interest is his 1962 book *The State and the Farmer*. It was co-written with University of Chicago political scientist Herbert Storing and contains a lengthy chapter examining the public interest emerging from British agricultural policy.[26] Storing, like Self, wrote other works examining debated concepts of the public interest in different contexts.[27] Storing locates the origins of what we term the public interest in modern liberal political philosophy where theories of individual rights were formulated to protect valuable individual interests against predatory rule. Liberal political philosophy pushed back against traditional notions of the common good which are liable to misleading and malevolent use by defective governments to threaten individual rights. The result is that our language of the public interest is typically expressed in individualist rather than communitarian models of politics. In essence, these models are used as a reactive and minimalist safeguard against either bad *theories* of government (such as delusions of communitarianism) or simply bad *practices* of government (such as corruptly self-interested rulers). Accordingly, Storing notes that 'a kind of tired cynicism' hovers around most of our use of the public interest as we try to defend a very minimal level of legitimate 'publicity' in our systems of politics and governance.[28]

A prevailing tendency in contemporary political studies is to reduce traditional respect for concepts like the public interest by increasing regard for the diversity of interest groups generally.[29] Henry Parkes can be re-framed in this context. The revisionist view is that Parkes is viewed as defending not *what he said*: the distinctive role of parliament as a deliberative assembly to determine the public interest; but rather *what we mean him to say*: the sectional interests of my group of elected members are more valuable to me than are the sectional interests of each and every group of public servants. What is denied to 'the public' (that it has a general interest) is granted to each and every self-interested group. Even more radical perspectives promoting individualism will go further and deny to these self-interested groups (that they have a shared interest) what it then grants to self-interested individuals.

Alternative approaches defend the relevance of public interest concepts and consider them necessary if and when a society wants to manage inter-group competition and rivalry. Some concept of a public interest is required when adjudicating interest-group rivalry, unless we simply pick and choose as the winner whichever interest groups happen to suit our own particular interests. We know that ministers and public servants would be under-selling their public interest obligations if they confined their interest to minimising interest group rivalry. The accommodation of prevailing interests falls short of the role government has in promoting long-term social interests through such policies as public health and public schooling. So too, environmental sustainability is a good example where concepts of the public interest act as effective standards of the need for substantial intergenerational interest in the environment. In ways that might alarm some – but not all – political conservatives, neglected cultural values of no immediate interest to many pressure groups can gain traction through claims made about their public interest value.[30]

Conclusion

The public interest is a relatively modern term. It is used in describe what was traditionally termed the common good. Goods and interests can be quite different. Using terms like the public interest can keep alive distinctions between self-interested and other-interested conduct in modest but important ways consistent with many of the sounder cultural norms of modern political liberalism. Self and Storing each make good cases that rehabilitating the language of the public interest can serve a surprising productive purpose. They have foremost in mind the re-education of the civil service in its leadership roles and responsibilities. The emphasis is on statecraft or, indeed, 'statesmanship' which is an increasingly neglected aspect of contemporary democratic governance, especially among elected politicians who think more closely of the electorate that gave them authority than the state through which they exercise power.[31]

Endnotes

1. Michael Di Francesco, 'The Contract State and the Public Interest', in Dennis Glover, Glenn Patmore & Gary Jungwirth (eds), *For the People: Reclaiming Our Government*, Pluto, Sydney, 2000, pp. 43–55; Richard Mulgan, "Perspectives on 'The Public Interest,'" *Canberra Bulletin of Public Administration*, no. 95, 2000, pp. 5–12. I acknowledge the research assistance of James Frost in the completion of this chapter.
2. Robert E Goodin, 'Institutionalizing the Public Interest: The Defense of Deadlock and Beyond', *American Political Science Review*, vol. 90, no. 2, June 1996, pp. 331–43.
3. For example see Jeremy Bentham, *Bentham's Handbook of Political Fallacies, Revised and Edited by Harold A Larrabee*, Harold A Larrabee (ed.), Harper Torchbooks, New York, 1962, pp. 98–99, 229–34.
4. Henry Parkes, *Fifty Years in the Making of Australian History*, Longmans, Green and Co., London, 1892.
5. Parkes, *Fifty Years in the Making of Australian History*, p. 391.
6. Parkes, *Fifty Years in the Making of Australian History*, p. 389.
7. Parkes, *Fifty Years in the Making of Australian History*, pp. 391–92.
8. Parkes, *Fifty Years in the Making of Australian History*, p. 392.
9. Parkes, *Fifty Years in the Making of Australian History*, pp. 400–402.
10. John Uhr, 'Accountable Civil Servants', in Mark Bovens, Robert E Goodin, & Thomas Schillenans (eds), *The Oxford Handbook of Public Accountability*, Oxford University Press, Oxford, 2014, pp. 226–41.
11. Martin Gilbert, *Winston Churchill, the Wilderness Years*, Pimlico, London, 2004; Uhr, 'Accountable Civil Servants', pp. 228–230.
12. Gilbert, *Winston Churchill, the Wilderness Years*.
13. Gilbert, *Winston Churchill, the Wilderness Years*, pp. 107, 173, 267–68.
14. Gilbert, *Winston Churchill, the Wilderness Years*, p. 177.
15. Gilbert, *Winston Churchill, the Wilderness Years*, p. 184.
16. John A Rohr, *Civil Servants and Their Constitutions*, University Press of Kansas, Lawrence, Kansas, 2002, pp. 29–31.
17. For example see Winston S Churchill, *Marlborough: His Life and Times*, GG Harrap London, 1947, pp. 441, 477.
18. Gary Greenberg, *Revolt at Justice*, in Amy Gutmann & Dennis Thompson (eds), *Ethics and Politics: Cases and Comments*, Nelson-Hall Publishers, Chicago, 1984, pp. 80–89.
19. Greenberg, *Revolt at Justice*, pp. 83, 84.
20. Greenberg, *Revolt at Justice*, p. 87.
21. John Uhr, 'Ethics and Administrative Responsibility: Lessons from the Ponting Case', in Paul Keal (ed.), *Ethics and Foreign Policy*, Allen & Unwin,

Sydney, 1992, pp. 98–118; John Uhr, *Terms of Trust: Arguments over Ethics in Australian Government,* UNSW Press, Sydney, 2005, pp. 164–81.

22 Uhr, 'Ethics and Administrative Responsibility: Lessons from the Ponting Case', p. 105.

23 Uhr, *Terms of Trust: Arguments over Ethics in Australian Government,* pp. 173–77.

24 Peter Self, *Administrative Theories and Politics: An Inquiry into the Structure and Processes of Modern Government,* Allen & Unwin, London, 1972, pp. 178–79.

25 Self, *Administrative Theories and Politics,* pp. 284–87; see also Peter Self, *Econocrats and the Policy Process,* London: Macmillan, 1975, 121–22, 175–76; Peter Self, *Political Theories of Modern Government: Its Role and Reform,* Allen & Unwin, London, 1985, pp. 83–84; and especially Peter Self, *Government by the Market?,* Macmillan, London, 1993, pp. 232–61.

26 Peter Self and Herbert J Storing, *The State and The Farmer,* University of California Press, Berkeley, 1962.

27 For example see Herbert J Storing, 'The Crucial Link: Public Administration, Responsibility and the Public Interest', in Joseph M Bessette (ed.), *Toward a More Perfect Union: Writings of Herbert J Storing,* American Enterprise Institute, Washington DC, 1995, pp. 269–83.

28 Storing, p. 274.

29 John Uhr, 'Be Careful What You Wish For', in J Boston, A Bradstock, and D Eng (eds), *Public Policy: why ethics matter,* ANU E Press, Canberra, 2010, pp. 79–97.

30 Uhr, 'Be Careful What You Wish For', pp93-96.

31 For example see Self, *Administrative Theories and Politics: An Inquiry into the Structure and Processes of Modern Government,* pp. 189–299; Storing, 'The Crucial Link', pp. 282–83.

CHAPTER 8

Balancing competing public interests within the public sector

Geoff Gallop

I am a reflective practitioner interested in theory. I am also interested in practice and the real world that surrounds and drives it. Part of that real world, of course, is the idea of the public interest and the expectation that it will matter in the way we have governed.[1] Implicit in the republican notion of government is that it ought to be in the interests of the people and not just in the interests of a faction or a clique. How to ensure that is the case is the subject matter for political science and leads some to conclude that the only workable definition of the public interest in a representative democracy is what a majority in the elected parliament and government deems it to be, no more and no less.

In reflecting on this definition I am led to observe that there are minorities as well as majorities and a future and a past as well as a present. As the great philosopher of political liberalism, John Stuart Mill, observed, there can be a 'tyranny of the majority'. To that we might add, there can also be a 'tyranny of the present'. Whether or not the considerations that flow from this mean we should widen the meaning of the public interest or whether we should just regard them as justifying an alternative set of interests counter to the interest of a majority today remains a moot point.

Perhaps it is best understood as a case of 'competing public interests' of equal or near equal status. This will be the working definition applied in this chapter.

The executive branch of government

My particular focus is on competing public interests in the public sector. I am concentrating on the executive branch consisting of our first minister and his or her cabinet and the great machinery it has underneath it to manage the state including those agencies given the power to monitor and report on performance such as the auditors-general, anti-corruption bodies, human rights commissions and ombudsman's office among others.

In the Australian system which is based on elections that create a parliament from which a government is formed, there are two forms of accountability, vertical and horizontal. The government is 'subjected to accountability that is both *imposed upon* it from outside by citizens, and accountability that it imposed *upon itself* through public institutions empowered to restrain the political executive'[2]. Vertical accountability by the state to its citizens is accompanied by horizontal accountability by the state to its own agencies of accountability. In such a system the potential for conflict is everywhere and not just in the rocky relationship that can exist between a government and its agencies of accountability. Inevitably there will be factions within the cabinet. On occasion, these factions will be led by the first minister and others keen on the top job. To this tension must be added the potential for conflict between ministers and the public service, between central and line agencies, between the agencies themselves, and between the executive and other levels of government. Local governments have various responsibilities that adjoin or overlap those of the states, roads being a good example. Ideas, interests and egos are all involved.

All parties would claim to be representing the public interest in one sense or another. There will be a first minister claiming a right to lead, as first among equals. There will be a minister and his or her office claiming the authority to instruct public servants. The public service will insist on its responsibilities as an arm of government and not the lackey of a *particular* government. Central agencies will claim the right to represent the government in their dealings with line agencies while line agencies will assert the special nature and indispensability of the particular work they do in delivering services in the community. Accountability agencies will point to the powers they are given to scrutinise and report. Finally, there are those in the backrooms not seen but very much in the limelight if the computer system collapses or the wages are not paid.

Each has a function to perform or an activity to support with a complementary notion of what can or cannot be done. There will be written rules and unwritten rules and most certainly there will be politics which attempts to determine who gets what, when and how. In the political realm, some public sectors will be 'joined-up' and operate smoothly, almost machine-like, whereas others may be riddled with conflict hosting a war of all against all and no agreed rules in bringing people, resources and outcomes together. Personal capacities and political skills – particularly but not only from those in leadership positions – matter just as much as intellect and knowledge. How this network of relationships operates will have a significant influence on the community's shared quality of life. Its efficiency will impact on taxpayers, its effectiveness on consumers of government services and its integrity on the confidence of citizens in public institutions. The ideas and aspirations that the incumbent government brings to the discussion table matters. So too, the personnel who are selected to assist in bringing a vision to reality because leadership and management are needed at all levels. How the vertical and horizontal accountability works to pressure governments to act in agreed ways is critical alongside the quality of the information provided to legislators about what works and what doesn't. Put these three ingredients together and you have what I would call the Enlightenment Formula for Good Government:

Leadership + Accountability + Evidence = the Public Good

There's no one definition of what a good government should look like. Nevertheless, one would hope that whatever beliefs and opinions a particular party brings to government, that party will subject itself, and be subject to, the tests implicit in the Enlightenment Formula. Think of governments without ethical and effective leadership, governments freed from responsibility or accountability and governments disinterested in the findings of scientific research or independent inquiries. Setting an example, acting ethically, knowing that you are subject to scrutiny, and developing policy on the basis of evidence are what the public interest is all about. These ideas can be situated within the context of an abbreviated history of public sector management.[3]

Public sector management – a short history

In the years following the Second World War, the state occupied a powerful position in our society. The public servants who worked for it, whether in the big departments or government-owned utilities, had significant influence over the politicians and they wielded power in the community. The state participated in economic activity and delivered a range of services with the aim of ensuring social and geographic equity. In organisational terms the system was essentially a hierarchy that was separate from the many aspects of economic and commercial life that it controlled or regulated. These arrangements were all very understandable as the democratic state had defeated the fascist challenge and was held in the highest regard. But change was imminent.

Starting in the 1970s and peaking in the 1990s, the New Public Management revolution brought the business sector into the heart of government, with business people becoming advisers, service deliverers and managers. The private sector model featuring a board of directors, a manager and an executive team with the objective of maximising shareholder value was delivered lock, stock and barrel to the public sector. Big government enterprises were disaggregated and some were sold off. Those that were retained became commercial entities that were publicly owned but privately run. The major themes were virtually mantras: 'let the managers manage', 'contestability', 'the level playing field' and 'productivity'.

The New Public Management approach swept through the world and was exported to the developing world courtesy of many aid programs. It produced improvements but also problems for a sector that was ill-suited to well-meaning efforts to transform their transaction along private sector lines. For example, concern was rightly expressed that the entry of market principles into the regulatory and policing functions of government, where the prevention of market failure was a key concern, might endanger the public interest. Indeed, there was resistance to the wholesale application of market-based ideas. The eventual response was a philosophy of 'creating public value' as opposed to 'maximising shareholder value'. A range of activities was designed to promote the creation of public value. Coats and Passmore explained that

> public value argues that public services are distinctive because they are characterised by claims of rights by citizens to services that have been authorised and funded through some democratic process ... it is designed to get public managers thinking about what is most valuable in the service that they run and consider how effective management can make the service the best that it can be.[4]

The call was for a public sector that was community focussed rather than producer focussed and strategic rather than controlling.

It seemed so simple. The Right had replaced the Left and then a 'third way' located in-between the two followed. The prevailing thought went from a Strong State to a Market State to an Enabling State[5]. For the Strong State equity was a prime concern; for the Market State efficiency was a prime concern; and, for the Enabling State it was economic, social and environmental improvement alternatively described as 'the triple bottom line'. My dissatisfaction with this formulation is the encouragement to think there is just 'one system' and that a 'choice' had to be made about which system to adopt. The reality, however, is that there are, and there needs to be, elements of each of these systems in our contemporary practice. We need a 'mixed economy'.

Complexity not simplicity should be our working principle when it comes to finding the public interest within the public sector. I need to make three points in defending this claim. First, the public sector is not, of course, just one entity. Rather, its mandate involves different types of work: policy development, the delivery of services to the community, monitoring, regulating and enforcing and the provision of support services like information technology and financial management to government itself. Each of these activities has its own 'logic' and 'requirements' that mean what would be good for one sector (for example, tendering for the delivery of services) may not be good for another (such as the delivery of policing).[6]

Second, no nation, region or locality is ever completely homogenous. What works in one place or for one community may not work in another. Historical circumstance and local factors will heavily influence the allocation of priorities and discussions about which approach will or will not work. Indeed, being locked into particular 'models' may make innovative approaches like place management unthinkable.

Third, and as Henry Mintzberg has reminded us, relations between the government and the people vary according to the specific framework within which they are considered.[7] When considering our democracy, we speak of citizens with rights and responsibilities and subjects with obligations to their fellow citizens. When it comes to a government agency or service, however, we talk of customers and clients with expectations and needs. What we want from our police service will be different from what we will want from our election commissions just as what we want from a government-run gas company will be different from what we want from a government hospital. In a sense, we are all stakeholders in government. The notion that there is just one way of looking at and defining the public sector is as remarkable in its audacity as it is flawed in its application.

What these observations tell me is that designing a public sector based on the public interest is a complex and difficult business whatever the ends a government may have set for itself. A governing party never inherits a blank sheet of paper onto which they can draw a picture of whatever they imagine and believe can be brought into being. Incoming governments inherit a complex system of relationships and regulations that will have experienced both change and continuity. In the modern world it is more likely to be the former than the latter. After all, there is lots of money to be made by advisers and consultants who will always argue that change rather than continuity is required. Bringing the many elements of the public sector together as an efficient, ethical and effective sphere of activity requires leadership of a special sort, leadership that will have its ears to the ground about how the organisational arrangements are working and whether change is needed.

Leadership of this kind starts with cabinet, cabinet sub-committees and ministerial offices and then encompasses the way the public sector is established and functions. Will it be ministries, departments or agencies? Will there be many small agencies highly focussed on what they do or large, amalgamated agencies that are easier for ministers to manage and with hopefully, lower operating overheads? What role is to be played by strategic planning, joined-up government and performance management or is all of this a waste of time and resources with government being seen as a grand example of event management? The framework of accountability can vary too. How 'open' is an 'open government'? How 'responsive' is a 'responsive government'? Ideas like openness and responsiveness are pitted against traditional views about top-down executive power that some say is needed when change is resisted by powerful vested interests. There is also divergent thinking on the best way to obtain the information needed to ensure good outcomes. Should the government look to departmental advice, special inquiries, contracted investigations or assemblies of citizens randomly selected to give their opinion? Research capacity in the public sector and in the community generally is a public interest issue and how much it is valued in arrangements for public administration matter too.

It is inevitable that the manner in which these questions are answered will lead to a public sector that incorporates a wide range of ideas about what works and what does not. At play are political beliefs, managerial theories and functional realities. The big systems that attract the attention of academics and consultants are necessarily abstractions. Indeed, the battle to define public interest based reform needs to go beyond theory into the machinery of government where decisions are made and both values and interests intersect.

The battles within government

Closer examination of the possibilities but also the problems of public interest reform reveals the breadth and the depth of clashes that are based on institutional position. For example, there will be clashes within a cabinet or a ministerial office over expressions of the public interest as well as at the intersections between the institutions, such as where ministers and public servants interact, over the most efficient way to advance the public interest. There are vested interest groups in all institutions and it is not surprising that they will collide when the different parts of government are brought into close proximity. For the sake of the argument, let me call them 'parties'. In my experience four distinct parties are readily recognisable: the business and productivity party, the power and control party, the sustainability and outcomes party and the integrity party. Within each we can see shared beliefs, a common language and varying degrees of organisation capacity to pursue common goals.

For those in the business and productivity party, cost containment and resource efficiency in taxation and expenditure are the paramount goals of government. They may seek short-term measures to deal with a budget crisis, medium-term measures to change work practices or longer-term measures to share support services across the public sector as a whole. This party is concerned not just with day-to-day costs but also with investment in infrastructure and the need to spend where the cost benefit calculations prove best. They prioritise economic rationality and question decisions that seem to stand against what 'the market' dictates. Backing up their thinking in the real world of politics is an army of business associations, financial journalists and consulting firms. They point to what they see as an indefensible 'productivity gap' between the public and private sectors. Efficiency is their motto, Gross Domestic Product their primary indicator and treasury officials their base within government.

The power and control party puts its focus on whether or not what the government wants is happening. Their interest in public sector matters focuses on the appointment and dismissal powers of a government, their capacity to create a coterie of political advisers and the need for the centralisation of political and bureaucratic power rather than its devolution. They are interested not just in what is happening within government but how that is communicated to the outside world. It follows that information management is accorded a top priority in the way they arrange their affairs and this priority needs to be reflected in the way the public sector operates. Power is their motto, media management a key principle and the cabinet their base within government.

What I have called the power and control party practises to a lesser or greater degree what the late Peter Aucoin called New Public Governance and it involves 'the integration of executive governance and the continuous campaign, partisan-political staff as a third force in governance and public administration, a personal politicisation of appointments to the senior public service, and an assumption that public service loyalty to, and support for, the government means being promiscuously partisan for the government of the day'.[8] Given the political pressures that exist in modern democracy, it is a political tendency that is not going to evaporate soon, if at all.

The sustainability and outcomes party takes us to a higher level with their desire to ensure that what the government is doing is creating value for the community, whether it is jobs and income, peace and justice, environmental amenity or national security. They favour reforms like outcomes-based budgeting and performance management at all levels, including whole-of-government evaluation. They accept that there will need to be some overlap between government and civil society and, to that end, expertise in community engagement and partnering will be priorities. Many within the line agencies, particularly the larger ones, like the emphasis on outcomes because it gives them strength when seeking to convince treasurers and their advisers that they need resources for the achievement of specified outcomes. They are supported in these endeavours by schools of public policy and research institutes. Effectiveness in respect of the triple bottom line is their goal and evidence is their guide to good policy.

Like the power and control party, the integrity party is focussed on process matters but from the perspective of ethical practice and the avoidance of conflicts of interest. They want codes of conduct to clarify what is right and wrong, risk management systems to prevent corruption, and monitoring of activity within the public sector by independent bodies with wide powers of investigation. Integrity is their motto and they see efficiency and effectiveness as important but not at the expense of due process and public trust in government. The need for control is understood too but not if it leads to a blurring of the important distinction between 'party' and 'state' and the creation of inappropriate networks and partnerships. They have strong support within civil society, particularly the legal fraternity, but need to translate that support into adequate funding from government and a robust mandate from the parliament. Acquiring money and power is not always easy.

The power and control party and the integrity party are often at loggerheads over issues related to transparency and regulation. This is not surprising given that governments want the power to make things happen. After all, that is why they seek election. The integrity party on the other hand places a straitjacket around the exercise of power in all sorts of ways. But just as governments can cross the line between what is and is not acceptable, so too can accountability agencies engage in over-reach. They need common sense as much as those in government need integrity. There is also continuing tension between the business and productivity party and the sustainability and outcomes party. Governments are invariably caught in the middle between taxpayers seeking relief and citizens wanting performance.

At best these conflicts within the public sector represent a work-in-progress. These are, tragically, wars without winners. Each party has its ideologues, indeed they resemble fundamentalists, for whom complete victory is sought but not achieved in a society where the public interest remains intact as a question mark attached to all that we do. Governments should be able to govern but they must do so in a right and proper way. Jobs and investment do matter, as does the quality of our social relationships as well as the natural and built environment. It is a mix of these elements of government and policy that needs to be found for the public interest to prevail. Allowing the public interest to prevail requires a proper degree of trust across the party boundaries as well as each party having sufficient power and influence that their voice is heard when decisions are made. I have in mind both personal power and collective influence. Essentially what we need is a public sector that is consistent with the public interest, one that recognises the range of concerns that have to be met by a good government and embedding them into the power and influence structures of government itself.

The post-truth party

Of contemporary concern ought to be the emergence of a new theatre of war. It is being fought between the research wing of the sustainability and outcomes party and the new tribe of what I call 'post-truthers' over the very definition of 'evidence'[9]. It is the case that governments will necessarily find themselves seeking compromises with beliefs they don't share or with ideas they assume will be unproductive. What is evidence for some will be ideology pure and simple for others. This disagreement is the very nature of politics. In seeking the best we often have to settle with the second-best. But we need to avoid the situation where one set of beliefs are everything and there being no room for these beliefs to be tested alongside other beliefs or their modification in real-world application. This debate over knowledge and evidence has found its way into politics and government by a strange set of circumstances.

'Post-truth' politics sees itself as the voice of the people as against the experts and elitists who are hell-bent on imposing their will over and above the felt beliefs and everyday feelings of ordinary people. The necessary give and take between the four parties that I described earlier is considered by post-truth populists to be too compromising of the 'will of the people'. Of necessity it should be 'all take' and 'no give' by the power and control party. The battle that has emerged in contemporary politics is not over the right mix to achieve good results but over the very idea that such a mix is acceptable. Sometimes it is expressed in class terms and takes the form of we, the ordinary people, versus them, the elitist professionals. Sometimes it is expressed in national terms as our monochrome values versus multicultural values, and sometimes in political terms with we, the people, versus them, the political class. Imagine for example what happens to the Enlightenment formula when leadership means control, accountability is at best only vertical and the evidence of scientific inquiry is not considered necessary. The public interest is lost from sight and is unlikely to be protected or promoted.

If knowledge is self-defined, by which I mean knowledge is what we want it to be and no more, then it is hard to imagine any continuing relationship of trust between the various actors and institutions of government. It is one thing to have a discussion around the compromises that emerge as a result of the struggles between executive power and proper process on the one hand and between the economics of business and the triple-bottom line on the other. It is quite another thing to see ourselves swimming in a sea of self-defined certainties. This lamentable situation considers the public sector as 'pure instrument' and nothing more. It is certainly not a set of institutions built to facilitate government and to subject that government to internal as well as external examination on behalf of a range of requirements that include the economic, social and environmental as well as ethical. What the post-truthers are recommending is not a community discussion around the meaning and application of the public interest. Rather, they are questioning the very concept itself and undermining respect for proper process in knowledge acquisition, policy process and efficient implementation. They seek to unleash the executive from the restraints we have built over decades if not centuries, whether generated by research and science or by recognition of the essential plurality of existence and the contradictions it brings.

The prevailing situation and the evolution of new challenges to our polity pose questions for every citizen. To what extent are we to confront the contradictions and complexity of the real world rather than withdraw into the cocoon that is simplicity and superficiality? These are questions of character, of ethos and, most importantly of personal responsibility. As one commentator put it, the public interest is 'a kind of question mark' we put forward in whatever we seek to achieve and however we seek to achieve it.[10] Its importance is most easily understood when we contemplate a world in which it is destroyed or devalued. That is not a pretty sight.

Endnotes

1. For my general definition of the public interest see Geoff Gallop, 'What is the Public Interest?' *Public Administration Today*, vol. 12, July – December 2007, pp. 44–48.
2. Mark Schacter, 'When Accountability Fails: a Framework for Diagnosis and Action', *Institute in Governance: Policy Brief*, number 9, May 2000, p.1.
3. Some of what follows is adapted from my paper 'Putting the theory of public service into action', *The Mandarin*, 11 December 2014.
4. David Coats and Eleanor Passmore, *Public Value: The Next Steps in Public Sector Reform*, The Work Foundation, London, 2008, p. 4.
5. John Benington, 'From Private Choice to Public Value'; *http://www.cihm. leeds.ac.uk/document downloads/John Bennington Private Choice to Public Value.pdf*
6. See Geoff Gallop, 'Public leadership, public value and the public interest', *Public Money and Management*, vol. 31, no. 5, September 2011, pp. 371–76.
7. Henry Mintzberg, 'Managing Government, Governing Management', *Harvard Business Review*, vol. 74, no. 3, May - June 1996, pp. 75–83.
8. Peter Aucoin, 'New Public Governance in Westminster Systems: Impartial Public Administration and Management Performance at Risk', *Governance: An International Journal of Policy, Administration and Institutions*, vol. 25, no. 2, April 2012, p. 179.
9. Geoff Gallop, 'A Post-Truth World – What does it Mean?', *Australian Rationalist*, vol. 108, March 2018, pp. 19–21.
10. Terry Cooper, *The Responsible Administrator*, San Francisco Jossey-Bass Publishers, 1998, p. 77.

CHAPTER 9

The public interest and media reporting

Shaun Carney

There was no question about the purpose of my journalistic journey when it began on 23 January 1978 – my first day as a fourth-year cadet journalist at Melbourne's afternoon newspaper, *The Herald*. As I walked into the stolid greyness of the *Herald*'s newsroom, with its linoleum floor and standard-issue metal desks, each hosting a typewriter and a battered leather swivel chair, I believed that I was setting out on a career to preserve and defend the public interest. After all, I'd long believed that was what the media did.

With 40 years' experience behind me, how does the media's public interest mission look to be working out? My report card would read 'Just managing. Can do better.' Through the years I've luxuriated in convincing myself, and persuading anyone who asked, that I've been dedicated in my work exclusively to serving and enhancing the public interest. This has been a comforting piece of self-talk. But I wonder how profound the link between the activities of the media and the public interest will remain in the years to come.

The press – or as we now refer to it, the media – is not just an important element of a properly functioning liberal democracy, it is vital. Those of us who write for newspapers and websites or generate reports for broadcast media form the Fourth Estate. It is a term that resounds with importance and rightly so, despite its uncertain provenance. And it is generally believed that the term is predicated on the traditional European concept of the three estates of the realm: the clergy, the nobility, and the commoners. The press, as it developed in the eighteenth century, started to be regarded as a fourth element, or power, within the realm. In England it came into usage with the establishment of the reporters' gallery, empowered to report on the proceedings of Parliament, in the 1780s. Along with the Lords Spiritual, the Lords Temporal and the Commons sat the Fourth Estate, created to keep the elected representatives of the people accountable chiefly through the recording and dissemination of their public utterances.

In the modern context, the term is often used in a way that perhaps many of us who studied civics or social studies in high school will understand: the press is the fourth power, the other three being the arms of government that make, interpret and enforce the laws. Since the development of mass media, first through the establishment of mass circulation newspapers in the late nineteenth century and then with the establishment of television in the second half of the twentieth century, the media has devoted itself to much more than compiling straightforward reports of parliamentary debates. It has blended its responsibility to report the important goings-on within a society with much that the public does not, when you get right down to it, need to know. It might well be information that the public would like to know or even wants to know. But is it necessarily information that is vital for the best interests of the public to be well-served? And what is the acceptable balance between what we should know and what we want to know?

This is where the certitudes that motivated me in 1978 need to be revisited. I believe that in 2018, a useful method for us to consider the way that media reporting benefits the public interest is to recall an oft-used quotation from Lewis Carroll's novel *Through the Looking Glass*:

'When I use a word,' Humpty Dumpty said, in rather a scornful tone, 'it means just what I choose it to mean – neither more nor less.' That is to say, the relationship between the public interest and media reporting, which has always been fairly elastic, is becoming even more flexible: it is whatever the media says it is at any time. As the media landscape becomes more fragmented due chiefly to the rising dominance of digital communications delivery, the true mass audience becomes a thing of the past, and the scramble for an audience – any audience – becomes just that little bit more desperate. This inevitably influences what the media chooses to report and how it orders its offerings.

When you take a step back and consider the very nature of the media – how it came to be, its ownership structure, its reason for being – it is in many ways remarkable that the media managed for so long to retain its relatively high standing in the community, and for its products to have been regarded as compelling and necessary by so many citizens. After all, the various arms of the media – certainly the commercially-owned parts of it that make up the overwhelming majority of the media and even the publicly-owned Australian Broadcasting Commission and the Special Broadcasting Service, which in some aspects are there to compensate for areas of commercial market failure – have plied their trade via an informal but enduring and quite powerful social licence.

Journalists ask their questions as part of a trade-off: society allows them to poke their noses in other people's business and in return society is rewarded with unimpeachable information, assembled and presented from a default position that seeks to be disinterested. Significantly, the media decides what it will and will not look into. That is the essence of the media-public interest relationship in its most abstract form. It has always been a remarkable arrangement. Throughout my career I worked for publicly listed commercial organisations that were in the news game for a profit. The real money was in selling advertising. But it was the journalism that attracted the readers – specifically, the type of readers that advertisers wanted to reach. In the mass media journalism industry, base motives – the pursuit of filthy lucre – and high-minded motives – the pursuit and exposure of the truth – leveraged off each other and for the most part co-existed without too much trouble.

The businesses were built on trust. Other industries are also built on trust: medicine and the law are two, but practitioners in those fields must hold qualifications. There is no statutory qualification for journalists. Anyone can do it. Perhaps banking is the most comparable sector when it comes to provider-client trust but even that sector is subject to considerable regulatory oversight – as flawed as that might appear to be in the wake of evidence presented to the Royal Commission into Misconduct in the Banking, Superannuation and Financial Services Industry throughout 2018.

When it is asked 'what is it that reporters do?', the simple answer is that they either ask questions or witness events or look through data, or a combination thereof, then put the material together in either written form or in a format capable of being broadcast or posted online. Those are the simple mechanics of basic reporting. But how do reporters decide what they will report on? That is the critical question. It goes to the degree to which media reporting acts to benefit the public interest, to contribute to a better informed and more cohesive society. Every moment of their working day, reporters and editors are faced with choices – about what to cover and not to cover, and what to omit and include in their reports. Then they must decide how to order what they are producing. What leads the bulletin or the newspaper? Which pictures or graphics will accompany the stories? When and how do they decide that a running story has run out of puff and choose to no longer pursue it? And what does it take to get them interested in reviving the story? A list of similar questions – choices that are made within newsrooms every hour of every day about such things as taste, morality, relevance to specific audiences and cost just to name a few – could go on to fill this article.

It is the job of reporters to be the observers, to report what they see, what they hear. To inquire. To be there. To update. To follow the story. To be on the lookout for the new and the unusual. To present unpleasant truths, unwelcome truths; to report things that someone powerful does not want the less powerful to know. The truth is that many elements of, and many participants in, the media aspire to serve the public interest. It is a key motivation for many journalists and editors. They are driven by a desire to use journalism to contribute to a wiser society – to reinforce the best elements of the community, the best impulses of people. To employ the various clichés, they seek to shine light into dark corners, to speak truth to power, to hold the powerful to account. They pursue the truth without fear or favour and they mostly do this by being part of large, well-resourced media companies that have built up their authority over many years and have deep pockets to defend themselves legally. They operate under the maxim that drove one of the great Canberra press gallery reporters of the 1940s, Don Whitington: ultimately you might not be able to be objective but you should always strive to be fair.[1]

How does the media operate in the best interests of the public? There is a general view, I believe, that this is done chiefly through investigative journalism. Perhaps this is a legacy of the Watergate scandal or just our tendency – exaggerated in this time-poor, highly distracted, mentally cluttered age – to pay more attention to the big-ticket items, the blockbuster news stories that are elaborately presented and potentially have a big impact. Certainly, this view carries with it some justification: the current royal commission into misconduct in the financial sector could not have happened without the journalism of Adele Ferguson of *The Age* and the whistleblowers upon whom she relied for her reports. Similarly, the work of various journalists, including Joanne McCarthy of the *Newcastle Herald* and Barney Zwartz of *The Age*, on historical child abuse by members of the clergy led to a Royal Commission and a great reckoning on this issue in society.

This view does a disservice to more mundane journalism. It is possible that some of us see investigative journalism as the one element of traditional, newspaper-based media that must be preserved because we have not thought about the wider social value of the media more thoroughly. More often than not, the media adds to the public interest by doing the less spectacular, quotidian things: covering the courts, the local council, planning disputes, transport – public and private, road and rail and air – health, the law, education, workplace relations, the arts. Plus crime; we need to hear about the worst in our society in order to appreciate the best. All of the information you cannot readily get without someone else going out to get it on your behalf. Throw in the weather, too. Our Google Home can tell us what the forecast for today is but it cannot tell us about wider weather patterns. And there is sport too. Sure, they are games and an entertainment, but they play a powerful social and cultural role – witness the rise of female participation at elite levels across a range of sports in recent years – and the major sporting organisations are, increasingly, economically and politically powerful institutions. The media serves the public interest by running the risk of prosecution under defamation laws with its reporting. Journalists will very occasionally face court action when refusing to divulge sources in order to protect their anonymity.

Simply explaining difficult subjects – issues that are hiding in plain sight, as it were – through media reporting can serve the public interest. As Harold Evans, one of the most highly respected British newspaper editors of the twentieth century, remarked: 'to make clear things that are otherwise obscure is itself a virtue, so that would be a contribution to journalism'.[2] There is another unassailable and companion truth: journalism has always been, to a discernible extent, about grabbing attention and entertaining the consumer. The question facing today's media is: how much should entertainment and attention-seeking – journalistic fripperies, such as the latest celebrity diet fad, that are now referred to as 'clickbait' – drive its activities? The business models that have sustained what we now refer to as legacy or mainstream media are crumbling. The once seemingly unbreakable symbiosis between traditional news, features and analysis on the one hand and advertisers on the other is broken. Now, much more than ever, the media – and here I am thinking about not just the mainstream press but social media, which does traffic in news and opinion – must provoke and pander to build and sustain audiences. All too frequently, the pandering is directed to the fears, prejudices, obsessions and worst instincts of news media consumers.

The negative effect of digital disruption on the media's capacity and desire to benefit the public interest should not be underestimated. We have not seen the end of the disruption. In fact, we never will. While you are reading this, something disruptive will happen to and within the media. We might not recognise it immediately but this is a ceaseless process; like rust, it never sleeps. And it has profound implications for the capacity of journalism to act positively in the public interest over the longer term. Until now, I have given reasonable space to the good instincts of the media. But I am nonetheless bound to talk about the real-world consequences of what is happening.

In May 2018, reports started to appear in the Melbourne media of an ex-AFL footballer who was featured in an explicit video that had been in circulation for several days. The mainstream media – that is, reporters and their editors – had initially chosen not to report the existence of the tape. However, as word of the tape started getting around, 'blind items' – stories that outlined the basic details but did not name the player – started to appear on newspaper websites. The video was also circulating on social media. It quickly became clear to many thousands of people that the footballer in question was Brownlow Medallist and former Collingwood star Dane Swan. By the end of the day, he was named in online reports on newspaper websites. The story led the evening bulletins of the commercial news networks.

The paper for which I am a columnist, the *Herald Sun*, led with the story on its Friday front page under the heading 'Sex, Pie and Videotape'.[3] The public interest component of this story was not overwhelming. It can be argued that because it touched on the issue of privacy there was something beyond prurience informing the decision to publish. Swan had lodged a complaint with the police that the material had been disseminated without his permission. In August 2018, a 20-year-old woman was charged with offences relating to the capture and distribution of the video. A key point to bear in mind is that this was made possible by digital technology. Citizens who were not journalists or editors were able to distribute the video through social media accounts. The conventional media followed, reporting on the existence of the video, once their old conventions of restraint were broken. Now and forever more, everyone can be a global publisher.

The interest of the public in this instance was definitely piqued. This was Melbourne after all – the place where Australian Rules originated. Did many Melburnians want to know who this footballer was? Yes. Did the reports provide information that directly assisted citizens to better navigate and understand the polity, bureaucracy, economy or society, which is what we might regard as a strict definition of public interest reporting? Possibly not. Was the public interest damaged in some way through the publication and broadcasting of this story, which was dead by the following day? I do not believe so, as long as media organisations continue to meet their other obligations, which I believe they do. Prurience can be in the eye of the beholder. The decision by the *Daily Telegraph* newspaper in early 2018 to reveal that a former adviser to the married Deputy Prime Minister Barnaby Joyce was carrying his baby seems to me to have clearly been in the public interest. It went beyond being information that should have remained private.

But will the media be able to keep its eye on the need to never abandon its public interest obligations? There is a fair amount of by-the-numbers unoriginal journalism now. Commercial television news – one of the most popular outlets for news in this society – is now a cavalcade of crime and courts. The bulletins all too frequently lead with CCTV footage of minor crimes, fires, suburban neighbourhood disputes, home invasions, car jackings, service station robberies, with the occasional report from Canberra or state parliament. This is largely a question of resources and the need to hold on to viewers as people turn to their phones or streaming services and advertising yields decline.

In Canberra-based media commentary, in parts of academia, in sections of big business and certainly in the bureaucracy, there is great nostalgia for the 1980s and 1990s – a golden time of policy reform and intellectual exploration. 'Oh, for the Hawke-Keating years, even the early years of Howard-Costello', goes the refrain. Difficult, transformative policies were introduced, explained and implemented. The sky did not fall in. There were few, if any, interminable policy catastrophes. Certainly nothing like the carbon emission policy follies of 2007–18 and possibly beyond. Things were different then, in politics and in the media. Back then, the media had a lot of money, big staffs and big audiences. It had time and space to explain policies and to be open to new ideas. Significantly, these were the last decades before the Internet and mobile phones changed the world.

I hesitate to be too critical of the current situation. There is enough doomsaying around already. It is nonetheless worth considering what many might diagnose as the biggest problem with our national polity in the past decade. In my judgement it is the incapacity of governments of both political complexions to move much beyond crisis mode and actually explain themselves to the public and subsequently to get a good run at implementing their policies. Is this a symptom of the digital disruption of the media? Is it really possible that energy policy has been so fraught and intractable because the public never really understood an Emissions Trading Scheme or a carbon tax or Direct Action or, for that matter, the National Energy Guarantee? How should responsibility for that be divided between the politicians proposing those policies and the media that's charged with reporting, explaining and analysing them?

What about voters? It is important when considering the public interest to remember the public's obligation to keep itself informed so that it can act in its own best interests. Did the public try – I mean really try – to get their minds around the policies? Or did they allow themselves to be too easily distracted by their new devices featuring social media feeds, games and videos? So far no one has found a way towards a new, far-reaching, comprehensive form of modern media that can act as a big tent, as an agreed repository, as a meeting place for trusted information. For some time to come, this will not matter that much. The existing arms of the mainstream media – the papers and the ABC, the commercial television networks and a few commercial talk radio outlets – will be popular enough in an aggregated form to provide a net benefit to the public interest.

In the long run, however, society will need something new. I think we can say that philanthropy and citizen journalism and crowdsourcing – these have been proposed as possible ways forward in the recent past – won't be much help. The disrupted media landscape carries considerable upside. The Internet enables us to locate so much information either through search engines and databases or through publications from all over the world. To an extent, we have all become our own protectors of the public interest because we remain informed … if we want to be. But in other respects, we should be wary of what is going on and the potential for news to be managed by vested interests and special pleading.

You do not have to be too old to remember when the content of a federal Budget was tightly held and revealed only on Federal budget night. In the past couple of years we have witnessed the rise of a new model: the budget as a very long publicity rollout. In the days leading up to the delivery of the budget, we see judiciously leaked bits of the document appearing right across the media with hints of cheaper beer, goodies for middle-income earners, some relief for hard pressed families with children, and so on. A lot of the budget's content is known well before release. Exempt are the bits that are not 'good' news for voters. On its present trend line, the budget will soon enough be little more than a government public relations event. The days of the budget being a sober, coherent, economic policy document are numbered. The challenge for the media in coming years will be to decide if it wants to assist governments with this public relations rollout of selected 'goodies' freed of context rather than reporting budgets in their entirety with the taxes, charges and levies as part of the mix of financial measures, in a truly disinterested manner.

The future has already arrived when it comes to on-the-ground reporting in some suburbs and towns, as local newspapers and regional news services have either closed or been consolidated. I have seen this happen in my own inner Melbourne community. We used to have a very good local paper. Each week, it covered the goings-on of the local council and sporting teams, carried material about the local state and federal parliamentarians, gave space to their opponents who were seeking to unseat them at upcoming elections, and mixed that in with a bit of crime for colour and movement. If you had seen police cars with flashing lights in the shopping centre around the corner the previous Tuesday morning, for example, you were likely to find out what had happened in the next issue. It might only be a couple of paragraphs but it kept you informed about your neighbourhood and the things you might want to be concerned about. It helped to inform citizens about their community and was delivered to the letterbox of each home in the area for free, sustained by advertising, much of it drawn from local businesses. That paper is no more. So how do I know what my local members are doing? They now send out self-congratulatory public relations handouts several times a year. My local council? Same thing. I have no way of knowing what they are really doing, the good, the bad and the ugly, unless I spend considerable time and effort making phone calls, sending emails and attending parliament or the local council chamber. Once upon a time, the local paper used to do that for me. How do we advance our society without common, trusted, respected sources of information?

This question is also a conclusion. I have left it hanging because, like everybody else in the media business, I am not sure that I know the answer. I can suggest, however, that the media in its current form, with all its widely acknowledged shortcomings, is a little bit like the effects of ageing: it can be annoying and disappointing but living with them definitely beats the alternative.

Endnotes

1. Don Whitington, *Strive To Be Fair*, Australian National University Press, Canberra, 1977, p. 73.
2. Harold Evans, interviewed by Razia Iqbal, *The Documentary*, BBC World Service, 26 July 2018.
3. *Herald Sun*, 4 May 2018, p. 1.

CHAPTER 10

The public interest and disciplinary communities

Jane Johnston[1]

People have been grappling with the meaning of 'the public interest' arguably since the notion of 'interests' were first articulated as a political concept in the seventeenth century. The Canadian political philosopher JAW 'Jock' Gunn notes the term was previously used in legal matters and the discussion of positive rights. It eventually came to refer to all concerns, including how they applied collectively to groups of people.[2] Gunn explains how public interest groups mobilised for social action by the 1650s. He contends that 'the age of interests, in the sense familiar to modern political science, had arrived'.[3] In this chapter I will use Gunn's observation as a starting point for examining the place and function of the public interest in the context of disciplinary communities, such as those associated with the law, media, anthropology and accounting. In considering the different ways disciplinary communities have aligned themselves with the public interest it is possible to show that the concept has been used to pursue different objectives and to achieve different outcomes. This observation ought to prevent any expectation of a single or overarching definition or depiction of the public interest.

My observations are consistent with the broad public interest literature which suggests there is no simple way of viewing either 'the public interest' or even 'interests' more broadly.[4] As Gunn has observed:

> It is never easy to write of interests: protean and all-pervasive, definable at any level of generality, multiple and conflicting even within a single individual – their coherent description strains our command of language and forces us at time into dubious metaphors.[5]

Indeed, coherence actually becomes a stumbling block in any quest to determine or describe the public interest. The absence of a universal understanding was illustrated when the *Guardian* newspaper invited its readers to propose a definition and found no common ground across the 150 responses it received.[6] A more realistic approach to finding consensus was offered by the American political scientist Frank Sorauf in the 1950s: 'a concept as nebulous as the public interest invites not definition but absorption'.[7] In keeping with this thinking, my chapter examines how the concept of the public interest has been absorbed into many theoretical and practical disciplinary fields. I will look at how the public interest is addressed in different professions and how pluralist notions of the public interest might help us to better understand the working of modern democracies.

Public interest theory

A brief overview of the theories underpinning different notions of the public interest will reveal the nuances of these disciplinary perspectives. The complex nature of the public interest is evident in the many threads of public interest theory. There are four broad public interest typologies: the abolitionist, the normative, the consensual-communitarian and the process-pluralist.[8] With the exception of the abolitionist approach that wants the public interest expunged from vocabularies, the other three provide some insights into how the public interest can be applied in communities and disciplinary contexts.

Notably, while the typologies allow for some sorting of the vast array of thinking underpinning discussion of the public interest, they do not represent discreet or entirely separate silos of thought.

Abolitionist

The harshest critics of the public interest as a concept argue that it is too unwieldy, ambiguous, anachronistic and unachievable. This is due in large part, they contend, to its lack of scientific rigour. That being so, abolitionists have no interest in the public interest and want to see it excluded from philosophical discussion and political debate.[9]

Normative

This typology takes a 'common good' approach to the interests of the community as a whole. The American political philosopher Barry Bozeman commends this approach because it advances 'the public interest as an ethical standard for evaluating public policies as a goal public officials should pursue'.[10] Likewise, Michael Levine and Jennifer Forrence argue that public interest theory is both a positive theory about what motivates policy-makers and a normative theory about what *should* motivate policy-makers.[11] While it is useful to maintain the ideal concept of the public interest because it 'provides a benchmark – one approached but almost never attained',[12] the normative approach is criticised because its objectives are considered unattainable.

Consensualist-Communitarian

This typology focuses on majority interest or negotiated consensus. This approach is premised on minimal consensus and holds that it is necessary for the operation of a democratic society.[13] Consequently, 'anything that is in the long term detrimental to the majority of citizens cannot be in the public interest, unless it is essential to the protection of those individual rights included in the minimal consensus.'[14] By its nature, the consensualist-communitarian approach relies on governments having 'basic rules' and carrying out 'fundamental social policies' that are understood and followed by the majority of the citizenry.[15] The American philosopher John Rawls concurs with this approach. He argues that a society must have a 'common good conception of justice', a 'reasonable consultation hierarchy', and it must secure basic human rights.[16] According to this view, pluralism can undermine the single most important value in society, that is, the sense of being part of a whole.

Process theories

This typology comprises three fields, each considering how the public interest is served during the process of compromise or accommodation. It is interested in how many publics, rather than a single public, and how many interests rather than a single interest, are the necessary foundations for considering the public interest. Inevitably, there can and will be 'conflicts of interest' because individuals with divergent interest are involved. This approach highlights the need for officials to provide practical reasons and logical explanations for their decisions. The mere statement of moral principle is not enough.[17] Within this typology, decision-making processes are aligned with *aggregative, pluralist or procedural* theories.[18] The aggregative model sees the public interest equating with an alternative to government interests. Its limitations lie in an inability to provide a valid overall aggregation of interests and the highly subjective meaning of what is considered 'good'. The pluralist model sees the public interest as compatible with the idea of balancing interests and accommodating interest conflicts. The procedural approach is also premised on a set standard for balancing interests. It requires procedures to ensure pluralist groups are heard. The pluralist and procedural theories have much in common and can operate in tandem.[19] Importantly, the procedural theory speaks to how the public interest can represent *many* interests. In particular, the pluralist approach is explicitly about multiple interests, also comprising self-interests, being voiced in competition, and generally challenging any expectation that any *one (the)* interest must be sought. The pluralist and procedural approaches are consistent with how many disciplinary communities work within society, and it is to this combination that I now turn.

Disciplinary communities

While the genesis of the public interest lies in political philosophy,[20] and remains embedded within public policy, regulation and administration, over the last few decades it has emerged as a concept that can be used across a wide range of activities. In some disciplines it undergirds a major part of the practitioner's professional standing; in others it appears to be an off-shoot from the main body of disciplinary thinking. In general, it is used to make sense of professional problems or disciplinary work; has developed into a framework for reasoned argument, justice and public good; and, been considered an attractive alternative to mainstream or traditional ways of thinking. Anthropologists, for instance, have developed a stream of dedicated 'public interest anthropology' which examines the public interest in terms of culture and society originating from a culturally-informed, pluralist position.[21] Accountants have turned to the public interest to develop guidelines for business models.[22] Psychology has a dedicated scholarly journal called *Psychological Science and the Public Interest*.[23] Public interest law exists to represent social groups and interests that are under-represented in the courts and legislatures.[24] Public interest journalism is committed to reporting issues touching on the wellbeing of the whole society.[25]

A large number of disciplinary communities now use the public interest – either in practical, theoretical or aspirational terms – to give their activities clear objectives and consistent outcomes.[26] Not surprisingly, there are similarities in the way disciplinary communities align their professional practice with the public interest. This is a thread that runs through much of the literature across various disciplines including media and journalism, law, politics, policy regulation, public administration, anthropology, accounting, planning, psychology, economics, communication and public relations.[27]

The attention given to the public interest by so many disciplines reflects its ubiquity in law and policy, its associations with political institutions, governance frameworks, legal systems and visions of civil society. Broadly speaking, these disciplinary communities use the public interest either to define their engagement with their respective publics (for instance, anthropology and law), their contribution to a broader sense of the public interest within society (such as in journalism) or both. They are underpinned in each instance with the idea of 'doing good' for society and enhancing their discipline. Some expressions of the public interest are well known and part of everyday language, for instance, public interest journalism and public interest law. Others, such as public interest anthropology and accounting, have not 'claimed' the name in the same way nor achieved the same kind of prominence.

I will now examine some of these disciplines and how they use and align their practices, aims and philosophies within the term 'the public interest'. While they present differing perspectives and entry points into thinking about the public interest, their work not only expands our understanding of the plurality of the public interest and the processes by which it might be advanced, taken collectively they broaden discussion with a wealth of helpful practical examples. Rather than limiting our understanding by offering concise but simplistic definitions, they enrich our overall conceptual understanding of the public interest and its possible productive uses.

Law

Public interest is a central concept in the framing of laws as well as shaping the field of legal practice.[28] My focus is the latter. Those who practice 'public interest law' represent 'social groups and interests that are currently under-represented in the legal and political arenas'. The main impulse is correcting systemic bias within political systems and enhancing social justice.[29] Public interest law is often associated with aiding the poor, representing political and cultural dissidents and new radical movements, and furthering what would otherwise be neglected interests such as environmental quality and consumer protection.[30]

It is no coincidence that the vocation of the public interest lawyer emerged with the rise of 'public interest groups'. The main task was engaging in campaigns and activities that were designed to represent minorities and under-represented voices.[31] The most common tactics include counselling, lobbying, commissioning research, launching investigations, exploiting the press and mobilising community action.[32] Public interest law is sometimes synonymous with *pro bono*, community or not-for-profit law. An example in Australia is the National Association of Community Legal Centres (CLCs) that are 'are independently operating not-for-profit community organisations that provide legal and related services to the public, focusing on the disadvantage and people with special needs'.[33] Moreover, they undertake 'matters in the public interest'.[34]

Public interest law has been described as 'making pluralism operative' and that, theoretically at least, it enables all groups in the community to be heard and hopefully heeded.[35] While the practice is clearly more complex and marginalised communities sometimes find they are competing with other community organisations promoting their own side-lined constituency, the idea of public interest law reveals a deep personal and professional commitment to the public interest within the legal community.

Journalism

Public interest journalism is not unlike public interest law in terms of motivations and methods. It is generally aligned with analytical and investigative journalism and is readily distinguished from entertainment journalism.[36] A report produced by the Australian Senate on the *Future of Public Interest Journalism* in 2018 noted that

> the term 'public interest journalism' is regularly used synonymously with the terms 'quality journalism', 'investigative journalism' and

> 'accountability journalism' ... there is a crucial difference between journalism that serves the public good, and journalism that seeks solely to entertain.[37]

Other descriptions, such as 'independent from vested interests' and 'journalism that reports and analyses the institutions of democracy', were also included in submissions to the all party Senate Select Committee Inquiry that was established in May 2017. Notably, some descriptions of public interest journalism did not distinguish between different types of journalism or included citizen journalism and blogging as part of their account of what constituted public interest journalism. The Committee's report highlights how the largely unregulated environment in which journalism is practiced is struggling against twenty-first century media disruption and the 'disinformation' insurgence coming from fake news and click-bait generators. Non-news and partisan media releases that are made to look like independent commentary pose a substantial threat to public interest journalism.

Broadly speaking, journalism invokes the public interest in two ways. The first invocation concerns the reasons for reporting and publishing news. Put simply, information is power in a participatory democracy. Those who control the flow of information are able to shape the views and opinions of those who vote. Those who hold and seek to retain power resent reporting that is critical of what is said and done. They sometimes seek to prevent reporting that identifies failed programs or exposes corrupt conduct. In resisting intrusion and censorship, journalists will resort to a 'public interest defence' in legal proceedings associated with privacy, confidentiality and defamation. The second invocation of the public interest relates to media ownership and implications for diversity.[38] Democracy is debilitated when the ownership of media is concentrated and in the hands of those with commercial interests that are subject to government regulation or parliamentary oversight.

The first of these invocations embodies the journalists' relationship with the public (or publics) and shared commitment to the public's 'right-to-know'. In 2012, the 'right to know' became a matter of national importance in the United Kingdom following the *News of the World* phone hacking scandal and the subsequent inquiry into the *Culture, Practices and Ethics of the Press* (known as the 'Leveson Inquiry').[39] The inquiry heard that the public interest, when used as a media defence, should be regularly reviewed to ensure it reflects social expectations and community norms. In the subsequent report, a number of experts thought 'there needs to be a wider debate on the definition of the public interest, in particular, if it is to gain enhanced status as a defence in the courts'.[40]

The more recent Australian report, *Future of Public Interest Journalism*, also visited this idea and noting that 'even if there is no unanimously accepted single definition of public interest journalism, there are certain behaviours, institutions and principles that have been commonly cited when discussing its role and importance in healthy democracies'.[41] These objectives include detecting or exposing crime, serious misdemeanours and anti-social conduct; protecting public health and safety; preventing the public from being misled by a statement or action initiated by an individual or organisation; and, highlighting hypocrisy, falsehoods and double standards on the part of public figures, public institutions and in public policy.[42] During the Leveson Inquiry similar lists were supplied by the British Broadcasting Corporation (BBC) and the British Press Complaints Commission (PCC). These inquiries illustrate the complex environment in which journalism is currently practiced and the strained atmosphere in which public interest journalism seeks to operate against the backdrop of the diminishing commercial viability of the news industry as a whole.

Accounting

The Institute of Chartered Accountants of England and Wales (ICAEW) has developed what may be the first 'professional framework' for practitioners working in the public interest. It includes a set of criteria for evaluating how to judge the public interest, using transparency and balance as fundamental tools and promoting the view that the validity of the public interest rests with both 'a pattern of behaviour that builds up reputation over time, as well as information directly relevant to the proposal.'[43] The framework centres on key issues that need to be addressed by those faced with the challenge of justifying their actions in terms of the public interest. Assessing the public interest proceeds through a number of stages: first, justifying the credentials of those with the right to invoke the public interest; second, identifying whether something is actually a public interest matter; third, considering the relevant public and discerning what they want and whether their wants contrast with their needs or other pertinent constraints; fourth, aggregating sometimes conflicting inputs and coming to a decision; and, finally, implementing whatever action is considered to be in the public interest.[44]

The ICAEW suggests that

> the framework should be useful to anyone as a tool for challenge and relevant to any of the wide range of actions that are asserted to be in the public interest … the framework also has a role for individuals considering an action such as disclosure of a matter that would otherwise be confidential, in the public interest.[45]

It argues against a detailed general definition of the public interest. Instead, it advocates the need to look at variations in individual circumstances as a means of assessing whether a policy or decision will serve the public interest in terms of its impact on affected individuals. The ICAEW includes a duty to protect and promote the public interest in its professional code of ethics with guidance in three particular areas: the formal responsibilities and public expectations of accountants; the mechanics of identifying and addressing conflicts of interest; and, the factors to be observed in the determination of fees.[46] By developing a framework and then carefully explaining its application to members, the ICAEW has made the public interest a professional virtue. Unlike the legal and media professions, there is no recognised tradition of public interest accountancy. The ICAEW's framework is an attempt to enlarge the accounting professions contribution to society through a better understanding and a deliberate promotion of the public interest as a guiding practical principle for its members.

Anthropology

Public Interest Anthropology (PIA) has been described as 'a paradigm for learning, teaching, research, action, and practice within the field of anthropology'.[47] It reflects a late twentieth-century trend in anthropology and the emergence among practitioners to expand the practical utility of the discipline. The objectives of PIA include confronting the political system as part of the research process in the interest of correcting contemporary disorders; developing better theory by working directly with various publics and their interests rather than merely applying theory in areas of interest to practitioners; and, communicating the public implications of research to multiple audiences in the interests of effecting change.[48]

This thinking emerged from growing determination to bring together the different fields of anthropology after the 1970s. This unifying work continued into the 1990s and 2000s. Notably, PIA was not originally promoted as a new field of research and action. Its aim was to bring together many existing threads with an emphasis on collapsing traditional distinctions in research, theory, action and application while synthesising elements of past practice and current theoretical debate. The influential work of Franz Boas was instrumental in bringing about change. His research on combatting racism was central to the modern understanding of culture as 'pluralistic, holistic, non-hierarchical, relativistic, behaviorally determinist'.[49] Consequently, the principal focus on pluralism highlights a common link to public interest theory and thinking held by other disciplines.

PIA uses a service model approach to anthropology. It is a combination of service learning, civic engagement, multicultural sensitivity and critical thinking, advanced through more rigorous theoretical and practical understanding of multiculturalism and a commitment to 'problem solving in the interest of building a community-oriented moral order based on equal rights'.[50] This service model challenges the idea of 'doing good' when civic engagement practices lack the necessary multicultural awareness. In such instances, 'culturally insensitive individuals reproduce the very boundaries they believe themselves to be breaching'.[51] The PIA approach confronts issues such as pluralism and multiculturalism head-on as it provides greater clarity in understanding 'the other' as well as taken-for-granted concepts about culture through the medium of face-to-face learning.

For the PIA practitioner, these insights demand a 'hands off' or disinterested approach to competing interests:[52]

> it is essential for the public interest anthropologist to articulate in relation to whom interest is defined and to understand the ramifications of competing interests with respect to a specific problem and course of action. This is not to say that the anthropologist will serve all interests, but that serving one interest often implies considering another.[53]

PIA has influenced the wider discipline of anthropology in many ways. In heritage studies, for instance, the cultural anthropologist Kathleen Adams observes that 'in an era of increasingly contentious identity politics and growing tensions over whose narrative should predominate at heritage sites, public interest anthropology offers a valuable approach for scholars'.[54] It also demands that scholars expand beyond theory-building to consider the social impact of their work. In cutting across the sub-disciplines of anthropology, including theoretical, applied and practice streams from within the discipline, PIA brings anthropological knowledge to a diversity of publics outside the academy and has allowed anthropology to influence public policy in significant ways.

Conclusions and new horizons

The public interest plainly takes on various guises. Its shape shifts with context. It has been widely adopted beyond political theory and, as I have shown, can potentially inform and influence many disciplines. In an edited collection dealing with public interest communication, my colleague Magda Pieczka and I have continued this venture into 'uncharted territory'.[55] We argue that a pressing challenge for 'public interest communication' is calling to account expert communication practices that work at the sharp edge of interest politics and to support scholars critiquing the status quo in developing theory and interrogating practice environments. Not unlike the evolution of PIA, we turned our focus to the theoretical and practical interfaces of the public interest, in this instance from a communication perspective. In developing a framework for Public Interest Communication (PIC), we argue that communication is in a dialectical relationship with public interest-forming practices, whether enacted through the institutions of the state (such as the legislature or the judiciary) or through civil society. Like other scholars who have seen the huge potential of the public interest as a conceptual tool for advancing their disciplines, we will continue to explore links between the public interest and our field of communication.

Our approach is consistent with Barry Bozeman's contention that 'public interest theory never goes away. It changes disciplinary foci, it receives more or less attention from scholars, but it remains'.[56] Indeed, it continues to contribute to disciplines that have actively explored the ways in which a firmer grasp of the public interest will expand the practical utility of the discipline as a source of insight for identifying and solving real problems. More important than defining the public interest is its 'absorption' and the openness of practitioners to be 'confronted' by the public interest as Walter Lippmann proposed.[57] As disciplinary communities continue to confront, absorb and ponder the consequences of reflecting on the public interest in their work, it will identify new issues and challenges and sharpen the focus of research and understanding. There is much to commend in a remark made by the American political scientist Richard Flathman more than 60 years ago:

> the problems associated with the 'public interest' are among the crucial problems of politics ... we are free to abandon the *concept*, but if we do so we will simply have to wrestle with the *problems* under some other heading [original emphasis retained].[58]

Since then, the notion of the public interest has not been abandoned – far from it. Rather, it is the public interest's adaptability and malleability as a concept that has allowed it to continue to resonate, making it a useful tool for framing the important conversations that many disciplines and society more broadly need to have.

Endnotes

1. Excerpts of this chapter are drawn from two works by the author: J Johnston, *Public Relations and the Public Interest*, New York, Routledge, 2016; and, J Johnston 'The Public Interest: A new way of thinking for public relations?' *Public Relations Inquiry*, vol. 6 no. 1, pp. 5–22.
2. JAW Gunn, 'Interests will not lie: a seventeenth century political maxim', *Journal of the History of Ideas*, vol. 29, no. 4, 1968, pp. 551–64. Gunn argues of the adoption of the term into politics at this time. The public interest is also aligned with other philosophical concepts such as the common good, identified much earlier by Aristotle (384–322 BCE) Thomas Aquinas (1222–1274) and others.
3. Gunn, 'Interests will not lie', p. 552.
4. For example, see TM Benditt, 'The public interest', *Philosophy and Public Affairs*, vol. 2, no. 3, 1973, pp. 291–311; B Bozeman, *Public values and public interest: counterbalancing economic individualism,* Georgetown University Press, Washington DC, 2007; CW Cassinelli, 'Some reflections of the concept of the public interest', *Ethics*, vol. 69, no. 1, 1958, pp. 48–61; CE Cochran, 'Political science and the public interest', *The Journal of Politics*, vol. 36, no. 2, 1974, pp. 327–55; RE Flathman, *The Public Interest: An Essay Concerning the Normative Discourse of Politics*, John Wiley & Son, New York, 1976;

JAW Gunn, 1968; FJ Sorauf, 'The public interest reconsidered', *The Journal of Politics*, vol. 19, no. 4, 1957, pp. 616–39.
5   JAW Gunn, 'Jeremy Bentham and the public interest', *Canadian Journal of Political Science*, vol. 1, no. 4, 1968a, pp. 398–413, (412).
6   Organization of News Ombudsmen (ONO), 'How do we define the public interest', 11 June 2012, <http://newsombudsmen.org/columns/how-should-we-define-in-the-public-interest>.
7   Sorauf, 1957, p. 619.
8   See discussion about these typologies and the theories they incorporate in, for example, Benditt, 'The public interest'; Bozeman, 'The public interest: its meaning in a democracy'; Cassinelli, 'Some reflections'; Cochran, 'Political Schience and the Public Interest'; A Downs, 'The public interest: its meaning in a democracy', *Social Research*, vol. 29, no. 1, 1962, pp. 1–36; Flathman, 1966; D Meyerson, 'Why courts should not balance rights against the public interest', *Melbourne University Law Review*, vol. 31, 2007, pp. 801–830; Sorauf, 1957; G Schubert, *The public interest*, Free Press, Glencoe, IL, 1961.
9   See discussion in Bozeman, 'The public interest and its meaning in a democracy'; and the articles referred to earlier by Cochran, Schubert, and Sorauf.
10 Bozeman, 'The public interest: its meaning in a democracy', p. 89.
11 ME Levine & JL Forrence, 'Regulatory capture, public interest, and the public agenda: toward a synthesis', *Journal of Law, Economics & Organization*, vol. 6, 1990, Special Issue [Papers from the Organisation of Political Institutions conference, April 1990], pp. 167–98. (168).
12 Bozeman, *Public values and public interest*, p. 90.
13 Downs, 'The public interest: its meaning in a democracy'.
14 Downs, 'The public interest: its meaning in a democracy', p. 9.
15 Downs, 'The public interest: its meaning in a democracy', p. 5.
16 D Bell, 'Communitarianism', *Stanford encyclopaedia of philosophy*, 2012, at <http://plato.stanford.edu/entries/communitarianism/>, para 4.
17 See the article by Cochran and Flathman referred to earlier.
18 Bozeman, *Public values and public interest*; Cochran, 'Political science and the public interest'.
19 Bozeman, *Public values and public interest*; Cochran, 'Political science and the public interest'.
20 See the articles by Downes, Flathman, and Sorauf referred to previously..
21 F Johnston, J. Paley, P Sabloff, P Reeves, P Sanday, *Public interest anthropology: planning seminar, a program for research, teaching and action*, University of Pennsylvania, Philadelphia, 1997; P Reeves Sanday & C Jannowitz, , 'Public interest anthropology: a Boasian service-learning initiative', *Michigan Journal of Community Service Learning*, Summer, 2004, pp. 64–75 (p. 65 quoted).

22 Institute of Chartered Accountants in England and Wales (ICAEW), *Acting in the public interest: A framework for analysis,* Market Foundations Initiative, 2012, at < https://www.icaew.com/en/technical/ethics/the-public-interest>.
23 Australian Psychological Society, 'Psychology in the public interest', 2015, at https://www.psychology.org.au/community/public_interest/.
24 'The new public interest lawyers', *The Yale Law Journal,* vol. 79, no. 6, 1970, pp. 1069–1152.
25 Senate Select Committee on the Future of Public Interest Journalism, *Report,* Commonwealth of Australia, 5 February 2018, at <https://www.aph.gov.au/Parliamentary_Business/Committees/Senate/Future_of_Public_Interest_Journalism/PublicInterestJournalism>.
26 Johnston, *Public Relations and the Public Interest*; Johnston, 'The Public Interest: A new way of thinking for public relations'.
27 See R Garnaut, *Dog Days: Australia After the Boom,* Redback, Melbourne, 2013; J Johnston & M Pieczka (eds), *Public Interest Communication,* Routledge, London, 2018.; and my own work (endnote 1).
28 Here I mean the use of the public interest in the following way: in legislation, for example in the *Evidence Act 2006* (New Zealand) (Commonwealth) Section 68: Protection of Journalists' Sources, at <http://www.legislation.govt.nz/act/public/2006/0069/latest/DLM393681.html.> which reads: '*the public interest* in the disclosure of evidence of the identity of the informant outweighs ... *the public interest* in the communication of facts and opinion to the public by the news media'.
29 'New Public Interest Lawyers'.
30 'New Public Interest Lawyers', p. 1072.
31 The contemporary idea of public interest groups and law is commonly associated with the social movements and 'general social upheavals' of the 1930s and 1960s, see for example, P Schuck, 'Public interest groups in the policy process', *Public Administration Review*, vol. 37, no. 2, 1977, pp. 132–40.
32 'New Public Interest Lawyers', p. 1146–1147.
33 National Association of Community Legal Centres, at <http://www.naclc.org.au/>.
34 National Association of Community Legal Centres, 'Tell me about the CLCS', at <http://www.naclc.org.au/about_clcs.php>.
35 'New Public Interest Lawyers', p. 1070.
36 Senate Select Committee on the Future of Public Interest Journalism, 2018.
37 Senate Select Committee on the Future of Public Interest Journalism, 2018, p. 3.
38 In the Australian context, see R Finkelstein, *Report of the Independent Inquiry into the Media and Media Regulation*, 28 February 2012; Australian Government, *Convergence Review: Final Report*, March 2012.

39 Lord Justice Leveson, *An inquiry into the culture, practice and ethics of the press*, 29 November, 2012, at <http://www.levesoninquiry.org.uk.>.
40 Leveson, *An inquiry into the culture, practice and ethics of the press*.
41 Leveson, *An inquiry into the culture, practice and ethics of the press*, p. 2.
42 Leveson, *An inquiry into the culture, practice and ethics of the press*.
43 ICAEW, *Acting in the public interest*, p. 4.
44 ICAEW, *Acting in the public interest*.
45 ICAEW, *Acting in the public interest*, p. 5.
46 ICAEW, Guidance on the public interest: conflicts and fees, at <https://www.icaew.com/en/technical/ethics/guidance-on-the-public-interest-conflicts-and-fees>.
47 P Reeves Sanday, 'Public Interest Anthropology: Opening Statement', presented at AAA Symposium, *Defining a public interest anthropology*, 97th annual meetings of the American Anthropological Association, 3 December 1998, Philadelphia, at <https://web.sas.upenn.edu/psanday/public-interest-anthropology/public-interest-anthropology-opening-statement/>.
48 Reeves Sanday & Jannowitz, 'Public interest anthropology: a Boasian service-learning initiative', p. 65.
49 Reeves Sanday & Jannowitz, 'Public interest anthropology: a Boasian service-learning initiative', p. 65.
50 Reeves Sanday & Jannowitz, 'Public interest anthropology: a Boasian service-learning initiative', p. 64.
51 Reeves Sanday & Jannowitz, 'Public interest anthropology: a Boasian service-learning initiative', p. 65.
52 Johnston, Paley, Sabloff & Reeves Sanday, *Public interest anthropology: planning seminar*.
53 Johnston, Paley, Sabloff & Reeves Sanday, *Public interest anthropology: planning seminar*, p. 3.
54 K Adams, 'Public Interest Anthropology in Heritage Sites: Writing Culture and Righting Wrongs', *International Journal of Heritage Studies*, vol. 11, no. 5, pp. 433–439 (433).
55 Johnston & Pieczka, *Public Interest Communication*.
56 Bozeman, *Public Values and Public Interest*, p. 86.
57 W Lippmann, *The Public Philosophy*, Transaction Publishers, New Brunswick, 1989.
58 Flathman, *The Public Interest*, p. 13.

Postscript

Tom Frame

This collection has shown that Australians generally assume that public leaders, mostly politicians, both define and then defend the public interest whether or not they agree with what they are defining or defending. As a broad statement of principle this is a fair assumption. But when principles are applied to practical matters, the contributors have revealed that complication, complexity and controversy is usually not far away. Application of the principle becomes *complicated* because there is a need to explain what is meant by public interests and the question of who has the authority to define them. Application of the principle becomes *complex* because there is a need to consider constitutional precepts and the common law (where applicable) together with parliamentary procedure and administrative regulations that might actively restrict or inhibit politicians from initiating certain action irrespective of whether it serves the public interest. And application of the principle becomes *controversial* when there are rival versions of what promotes the common good and, therefore, what advances the public interest.

The preceding chapters have shown the whole notion of defining 'a' or 'the' public interest is difficult and demanding, especially if there is a range of options involving a clash of values within the community. Defining where the public interest might lie is *difficult* because any claim requires considerable substantiation, and it is *demanding* because there are many objections (real and imagined) that need to be addressed if disagreements over what constitutes the public interest are not to actually divide the public. Each of the contributors has shown that the term 'public interest' is readily used in a number of scenarios but is hardly ever justified and is very rarely explained. It is not that those using the term are lazy or indolent nor are they being misleading or deceptive. It is simply a matter of the term being used in circumstances where a long definition is not possible or when there is a presumption that the claim is reasonable when it is really contested. In the 'sound bite' age, describing the public (or publics) served by a particular policy or decision and explaining how the interest (or interests) of citizens are being protected or promoted requires more time and attention than is often available.

For example, government policy on raising the retirement age and delaying access to the aged pension ought to be explained in terms of the public interest. It is a complex matter generating a good deal of controversy with the existence of contrasting views on the optimum age. While a government press release might cite the public interest as a reason for setting the retirement age at 65, 67 or 70 years, at some point there needs to be careful analysis of the competing interests professed by the various publics who will be affected by a government decision. Treating the term 'the public interest' with respect will increase general acceptance of whatever decision is eventually made. As Chris Wheeler explained in his chapter, people are more likely to accept a decision that is not in their favour if they believe the deliberative process has at least been attentive to their interests. Any political party claiming that a policy advances the public interest when a more sanguine interpretation suggests its principal purpose is attracting votes risks devaluing the while concept and making the public interest an empty term with no continuing practical value.

Can members of the public be wrong about what serves their interests? Of course they can. Ignorance and fear play an important part in politics. Sometimes governments want the electorate to remain uninformed about the origins or outcomes of a policy. Sometimes oppositions mount scare campaigns to instil fear of possible unintended consequences of a proposed policy. Changing the government through elections is an imperfect test of the public interest but, in contemporary Australia, it is ultimately how the people decide who governs them and what they hope those governing might do on their behalf.

Can governments acquire special mandates allowing them to do certain things, usually unpopular or controversial, in the public interest? Yes and no. Political parties have policy platforms that they put to the people during election campaigns. They contain promises about what a party will or will not do when in office. If elected, the victorious party will claim a mandate to implement their policies and expect the opposition parties and independents to 'respect' the will of the people. This sounds fair and reasonable. But politics is not far away. The Goods and Services Tax (GST) debate in 1997–98 is a good example.

John Howard went to the electorate pledging to implement a broad-based consumption tax. This was a brave political move prompting strong opposition from the Labor Party that pledged to resist any plan to impose a GST. The Coalition won the election with a much-reduced parliamentary majority and claimed a mandate to introduce the consumption tax. Notably, it did not win the popular vote. Given the Coalition's claim that the election was effectively a referendum on a consumption tax, Labor secured 51 per cent of the vote and insisted the majority did not want a GST. The Coalition managed to secure the passage of the enabling legislation with support from the Australian Democrats in the Senate (because the government did not command a majority on its own). The government's specific mandate to implement its new tax system was highly questionable. It was certainly not clear and unambiguous. At least the Coalition had 'conferred' with the electorate about its intentions prior to the election and could say those who voted for the Coalition knew they were effectively voting for a consumption tax. Whether or not the prospect of the government introducing a consumption tax actually influenced how they voted is another matter. Most election analysts argue that it did not. But in this instance, John Howard claimed a mandate to act in the public interest and implemented a policy that most commentators now consider an indispensable source of public revenue. It might have been unpopular but economists argued that it was good public policy and credit the Howard Government with determination and courage.

In sum, governments have the power (within the law) to pursue their policies noting the checks and balances (or the hurdles and hindrances) that our system of government maintains to prevent the rise of absolutism and the possibility of tyranny. The government is not omnipotent. Australians appear to like a bicameral system of government. Preferring to have 'a bet each way', they will vote for one party in the lower house and another in the upper house because they want to see government held accountable. It seems Australians want policy to be reviewed and refined before it becomes law. Is this frustrating? At times, yes, because a minor party or an independent can resist the will of the elected government and essentially the majority of the electorate. But it requires negotiation and that can help and hinder policy outcomes. It's never a case of always the one and never the other. Legislative amendments can be good and bad, positive and negative. The need for compromise means the government is constrained in the ways it can act and, for the greatest part, the citizenry appreciate these limits. The net effect is dispersing authority for determining the public interest and, theoretically at least, allowing more relevant considerations to inform definitions of the public interest. But does the involvement of political parties skew or distort these definitions more often than not?

A political system like Australia's needs political parties to avoid the chaos that would flow from, in the case of the federal parliament, 150 independents each pursuing their own version of the common good. The current system could not cope with reconciling the full range of possible views on what is practical and possible, quite apart from evaluating what is ideal and beneficial *to all*. The party system is, in part, an efficiency tool. In most communities, there is a convergence of views around widely prevailing opinions and aspirations, values and virtues. Political parties stand for the aggregation or conglomeration of these views. Each of the substantial parties in the Federal Parliament, the Liberals, the ALP, the Nats and the Greens, have a range of views within their respective memberships – they have conservatives and liberals, progressives and radicals. These parties canvas the spread of views held by, and this is a rough approximation, perhaps 95 per cent of the Australian people and can represent those views in the Federal Parliament. The difficulty is, however, shifting sentiment within these parties and the rise of independents and minor parties that have extended the political spectrum in both directions – left and right.

The readiness of the electorate to change its mind is reflected in the volatility of voting behaviour over the past 20 years. Not only has the combined vote of the two major parties declined from around 90 per cent of the total vote cast to around 70 per cent, swings of 20 per cent (especially in state elections) are no longer rare. The electoral mood is more fluid as the well-established parties know they cannot assume a natural constituency with rusted-on support. Party loyalty is low and swinging voters are unpredictable especially in the Senate and in the allocation of non-first preferences. The problem is not that parliaments are unrepresentative. The challenge is a fickle electorate. Voters are uncertain and inconsistent about what they want at a time when the policy options promoted by the substantial parties are converging and not diverging. Modern communications, the 24 hour news cycle and the growth of a 'commentariat' has made it much more possible for the electorate to convey their views to the political class. The challenge is reading the mood and, in many instances, persuading the people of the need for difficult decisions in the public interest that might involve some disadvantage. Hence, the frequency with which politicians mention the public interest – as though they know what it is and stand ready to serve it.

I would contend that decisions relating to the economy and personal financial self-interest are the ones that tend to galvanise whole sections of the community for or against the government. If there is a divide, it is the growing divide between the governing and the governed as discernible groups. The memberships of political parties are no longer active in policy development. Candidates are selected from a pool dominated by political staffers, industry lobbyists and union officials. Workplace inexperience and the narrowing professional expertise of parliamentarians has led to 'anti-politicians' coming to the fore. The anti-politicians contrast their lack of political experience with their practical exposure to 'real world' issues and problems. Parts of the electorate have become disenchanted with party hacks and products of the party machine and deliberately chosen candidates who are disruptive and whose policies are discordant. This may be Australia's version of voting for Donald Trump or Brexit. Is this an instance of the political landscape finding a new equilibrium? It is too early to tell. Geoff Gallop's chapter suggests that major changes are looming and in some areas reform should not be resisted.

Who defines, determines or decides what is in the public interest – in terms of policy? In theory, the responsible minister who is responsible to the cabinet, to the party room, to the party membership, to the parliament, the press and, eventually, to the people. If the national interest concerns the observance of a procedure – the minister must make decisions within the Constitution, consistent with state and federal law – and Australia's international responsibilities as a signatory to hundreds of protocols and statutes, and do so in manner that honours the demands of integrity and probity, and upholds natural justice, procedural fairness and expectations that taxpayer's money is well and wisely spent. The Government is constrained by laws and conventions that preserve the rights, freedoms, liberties and entitlements of individuals. The government can compel citizens to pay taxes and charges, to provide information and abide by rules and regulations but its authority is prescribed by law and its powers limited by conventions quite apart from the need to secure the general consent of the people for its policies lest its lose the electoral mandate required to remain in office.

This might lead to the conclusion that people in governments are managers rather than leaders: managers being people who make decisions about the effective and efficient allocation of resources to activities that have been imagined and implemented by leaders who have a vision of the future and how it can realised. Given that government is so regulated and that around 80 per cent of what government must do is fixed (that is, the provision of services and payments that exist regardless of who is in power), is it reasonable to expect parliamentarians to lead or merely to manage forces and factors that have a momentum of their own and which resist major changes in direction? In other words, are they just tinkering at the edges? There is something in this lament. In a pluralistic, multicultural, liberal democracy with a very large educated middle class, there will always be a competing array of claims and convictions about what constitutes the public interest. Because there are many views, governments hoping to gain the confidence of the people will come to a firm mind, show strength, demonstrate resolve, accept opposition and remain committed to a policy. The people will judge the policy and its pursuit.

As John Howard maintained while prime minister (and it was a stance from which he rarely deviated), politics is not a public relations exercise. It is casting a vision of the future that promotes the common good in the public interest – and leaving the people to decide whether the vision was clear, the common good was enriched and the public interest was served. Governments will inevitably get things wrong. None of us can predict the future with complete reliability. There must be some latitude for mistakes and miscalculations. But the present mood is unforgiving and unrelenting. National leadership is becoming increasing complicated, complex and controversial given the intense scrutiny applied to every government policy or procedure. These challenges are not restricted to parliamentarians who have created institutions, agencies and offices whose task is to ensure that where the public interest is defined in legislation every public official and every person in a position of public trust acts in the public interest. The task of protecting and promoting the public interest is now dispersed among public servants, the uniformed services (including the Australian Defence Force, the state and federal police and emergency services) and contractors acting on behalf of the government in the delivery of utilities such as water and electricity, and community services such as corrections and education.

As Jane Johnston has shown, a number of academic disciplines and professional vocations have embraced the public interest as an organising principle for their work. This is a welcome development that guards against expertise and experience being corralled within a particular self-serving sub-group and its practitioners becoming isolated from the society they are intended to serve. In these settings, the term public interest denotes different intentions and practices. There is variation in use but, I would contend, a shared commitment to others rather than self, and providing a benefit to the undifferentiated community rather than merely meeting the needs of the discipline or vocation. A concern for the public interest is having a renewing effect in the academy and among the professions.

Fortunately within the universities no faculty or department has managed to capture research and teaching on the public interest. Schools of business and government give the impression that the topic really belongs to them. Economics sometimes presumes the public interest will ultimately be determined in financial terms. Politics sometimes assumes policy debates are usually settled by election outcomes. Thinking more expansively, most disciplines have a role in defining, determining and describing the public interest. Philosophy can be helpful in differentiating interests from imperatives; sociology can help in discerning the consequences of a policy on community life; and, communications can help in assessing reactions to policies and decisions. Inasmuch as the public interest touches on all aspects of a nation's common life, the ideas and insights that flow from broad-ranging intellectual inquiry will help to sharpen the focus of public interest conversations and broaden their application. Each discipline has an important part to play in making the public interest a means of sifting and sorting competing claims about how human civilisation might be protected and advanced.

If the term public interest is marginalised in political discourse and lost from public administration, there are few things to replace it. The common good might be an alternative but it comes with its own category complications as Andrew Cameron has shown. Plainly, the issues raised and questions posed in this book have a personal and professional dimension for every parliamentarian, public servant and community leader. The conversation about the public interest is far from ended. In fact, it has just begun.

www.ingramcontent.com/pod-product-compliance
Ingram Content Group UK Ltd.
Pitfield, Milton Keynes, MK11 3LW, UK
UKHW021329180426
11947UKWH00017B/1532